LOOK FOR THESE

MW01097223

The Best of FATE Series

Psychic Detectives and Psychic Crimes
UFOs and Close Encounters
Angels and Heavenly Encounters
Psychic Healing and Spiritual Healing: Cases of Miraculous Recoveries
More titles in preparation

FATE Magazine Library of the Paranormal and the Unexplained

The World's Strangest True Stories
The World's Strangest True Mysteries
The World's Strangest True Experiences
More titles in preparation

FATE, LIBRARY OF THE PARANORMAL AND THE UNEXPLAINED

THE WORLD'S STRANGEST
TRUE ENCOUNTERS

SELECTED AND ARRANGED BY
PHYLLIS GALDE
JEAN MARIE STINE
AND THE
EDITORS OF FATE

FATE Magazine, Inc.
Produced by Digital Parchment Services

CONTENTS

TO

Frank Edwards
(1908-1967)
A good writer and a good friend of FATE

June - 2022

I WITNESSED A MIRACLE HEALING

Sam Diaz Pumara
As Told to Hazel I. Diaz Pumara

Are certain individuals so blessed that they can cure sickness by incantation alone? Are words, accompanied by puzzling ritual, sufficient to cure an ill man when all methods of medical science have failed?

There was a time when I would have said no to both these questions. Today I answer with the account of my personal experience. I witnessed a miracle healing—a miracle healing accomplished by the use of words over a sick man.

In 1932 my parents, my brother and I lived on an *estancia* about 60 miles west of Buenos Aires, Argentina. We raised cattle, linseed, and corn. My experiments in electronics kept me busy much of the time, so the bulk of the work was carried on by my father and my younger brother, Dick. The work was heavy, for in those days *estancieros* in Argentina did not have labor-saving farm machinery.

Dick was normally a very slender person. When the summer became exceedingly hot he drank large quantities of water, wine, and beer. Before the harvest was over Dick began to complain of pain in his stomach.

Over a period of time we consulted all the doctors within our reach, without relief for Dick. We took him to general practitioners and to specialists in Buenos Aires City, within the bounds of our income. Even the specialists recommended only an elastic abdominal support; they said he had a fallen stomach.

Dick bought the prescribed support but it only made him feel worse. Within two weeks he could eat nothing. Water made him sick. An hour after he tried to eat, his head would begin to ache violently.

Finally the only thing the doctors could recommend was complete rest with his body at an inclination of 10 degrees. It was hoped that his fallen stomach would right itself with rest.

By this time it wasn't difficult to get Dick to rest. He had grown thinner and weaker, with headaches increasing in intensity and duration until they were constant.

Nothing seemed to help and we practically gave up hope. We resorted to prayers.

One day a handsome young gaucho came to the *estancia* to talk to father about our herd. We had known Julio for some years and respected his opinions as much as we valued his friendship. When lunch time came Julio gratefully accepted Father's invitation to eat. It was at lunch that he caught sight of Dick. Unable to eat, Dick nevertheless came to the table.

"My friend, what is wrong?" asked Julio.

We explained Dick's illness and the hopelessness of the situation as far as help from the doctors was concerned. Before we had finished our story Julio stopped us. "I know of someone who can cure Dick," he said earnestly.

"Who?" we all asked in unison.

"I know an old man, a *curandero,* who lives not far from here. All he does is say religious words to you and pronto, you're cured."

The name *curandero* must have brought the same thoughts to my family as it did to me. Our religion had not actually taught us that the age of miracles was long gone, but such was the unspoken teaching which was everywhere evident among the religious people of Argentina.

Who in Argentina had not heard rumors of the marvelous healings of the *curanderos* and who had not openly or secretly ridiculed them? *Curanderos* were usually very poor, nearly always uneducated persons who reputedly healed by the use of words. No one called the words prayers. They were just *palabras.*

A few persons had told us they had seen *curanderos* heal the sick. But we were educated and considered ourselves intelligent folks who deplored the ignorance of those simple ones who believed that words alone could heal.

But Julio was insistent. "Dick, I am going to take you to see this *curandero.* If you don't come willingly I will take you by force. I know that he can cure you.

We of Spanish ancestry pride ourselves on our gracious diplomacy. One does not offend a guest if offense can be avoided. When we saw Julio's determination we knew that we must accept his offer. Then, too, we were desperate to find help for Dick.

That same afternoon, Dick, Julio, and I drove Father's car 30 miles across rich farmland, on dusty dirt roads, to the old man's house which was set at the edge of a corn field.

Julio called, "Don Juan, are you there?"

From the corn field came a voice, "Here I am."

In a few moments an aged Italian came from the field to greet us. He was about 70 years old, we learned later, but the hard life of poverty had left its mark on his face and stooped body. He looked ancient. His faded trousers were patched, and the patches were torn. His shirt was tattered and his feet were bare. Around his waist he wore a black *faja,* a width of wool which Argentine laborers wrap round and round their waists to support their vital organs from the strain of heavy lifting.

"What brings you here?" he asked Julio.

"I'm bringing you a sick friend who needs your help." "Come in, come in," said Don Juan, waving us towards his little house.

It was a three-room house without plaster on the walls. The brick floor was dusty where many of the bricks were broken out and missing. The furniture was scarred and broken. We went to the kitchen where Don Juan motioned for Dick to sit on a small three-legged stool.

"You will be cured by a Power beyond my power. It is the power of God," he said.

Don Juan removed the *faja* from his waist and substituted a rope to hold his trousers in place. He gave one end of the *faja* to my brother. Dick held the end of the two-yard length of wool in his right hand, close to his chest as Don Juan instructed him. Don Juan held the other end of the *faja.* He measured again the same length. As he was measuring and folding, he repeated words which sounded as though they might be Latin. The only words I recognized were "God," "Mary," and "Christ."

In the midst of this ritual, Dick turned to me and winked, as though to say, "Imagine such silly stuff!"

I was perplexed. Why should our friend, who certainly knew better, bring us to such an ignorant old man? How could anyone believe that folding a piece of wool while saying some unintelligible words would cure a fallen stomach? It was absurd. I finally excused myself and walked outside of the house.

I was amazed when I reentered the kitchen to find Dick as white as chalk. He was complaining of severe pains in his stomach. The old man was still muttering. Suddenly Dick's pains disappeared as quickly as they had come.

Now the old man took his *faja* from Dick and wrapped it around his own waist again.

"You will be all right," Don Juan said to Dick. "But for two days eat nothing but soup and boiled potatoes. The following days eat everything that is put on your plate."

Dick said, "Impossible, I haven't even been able to drink water. How can I eat food?"

Don Juan answered quietly, "The power of God is great. Do not ignore it!"

Dick rose from the stool and came to where I was standing with Julio. "A strange thing did happen while he was saying those words. I felt for a moment as though my stomach was going to be pulled right out of my mouth," he said. Then he suddenly touched his forehead. "My headache! It's gone. My God, something has happened! It is the first time in months that my head has not ached. It is absolutely clear." The look on his face was one of complete amazement.

Don Juan refused payment. "We cannot take money for these things," he said. "If we do, the Power sent to us will vanish immediately."

We walked to the car and Dick, who had been too sick for months to drive, asked to drive home.

We thanked Don Juan again and started for home. We hadn't gone half way when we saw a beer garden along the roadside. "I'm going to stop for a beer and some cakes," Dick announced.

"You can't risk it," I said, and Julio tried also to talk Dick out of stopping. We reminded him that Don Juan had told him to eat nothing but soup and boiled potatoes for two days. But Dick was determined and told us that he was hungry, so hungry that he would take a chance on more pain and discomfort.

In the beer garden we ordered beer and cakes. As I saw the order placed before Dick I was sure that this would be a real tragedy. We watched Dick consume the large draught of beer, ravenously eat the cakes and call for more. We returned to the car and started home. Dick still felt wonderful.

When we arrived home our parents were waiting and eager to hear what had happened. They were surprised to see Dick driving the car. I told them my impressions of our experience. Dick told them his, and Julio added his assurances that the cure was permanent.

Finally Father said, "If all you say is true, and it seems it is, a miracle has happened."

After two days of eating soup and boiled potatoes under Mother's watchful eye, Dick still felt perfectly well. The third day he called for a huge serving of fried eggs and afterwards ate a complete meal of roast beef and vegetables.

We all waited and watched, expecting every moment to see Dick double up with pain. But he continued to get better. His strength returned, his color was good and his whole outlook became optimistic and cheerful.

Don Juan had spoken the truth when he said that from the day of his cure, Dick would be all right. The healing took place 25 years ago and never once have any symptoms of a fallen stomach or its resulting distress recurred. Today Dick's health is wonderful, no complaints, no ailments.

So you see, a sick man can be healed by words spoken to God. I know this is possible, I saw it happen.

W. T. STEAD'S MYSTIC MESSAGES

Pauline Saltzman

The red-bearded, somewhat stoop-shouldered editor of the *Review of Reviews* sat wearily at his cluttered desk. His Mowbray House office in the Strand seemed a hectic place, and William Thomas Stead found himself unable to concentrate on his editorial work. He had just remembered that here it was late Monday afternoon; on Wednesday he was to dine with a woman friend, provided she had returned to London from Haslemere where she had spent the weekend.

Wondering what her plans might be, Stead took up a pen and placed it on a sheet of paper. Though his personal interest in psychic research had monopolized most of his adult life, he never had had a "psychic experience." Now, to his utter disbelief, his hand wrote, of its own accord, this message:

"I am very sorry to tell you I have had a very painful experience of which I am ashamed to speak. I left Haslemere at 2:27 p.m., in a second-class carriage in which there were two ladies and one gentleman. When the train stopped at Godalming, the ladies got out and I was left alone with the man. After the train started he left his seat and came close to me. I was alarmed and repelled him. He refused to go away and tried to kiss me. I was furious. We had a struggle. I seized his umbrella and struck him but it broke, and I was beginning to fear he would master me, when the train began to slow down before arriving at Guildford station. He got frightened, let go of me, and before the train reached the platform he jumped out and ran away. I was very much upset. But I have the umbrella."

Stead was flabbergasted, and not a little apprehensive, that his subconscious mind was responsible for the message. He wrote his friend a hasty note, relating the circumstances, and added how sorry he was about the embarrassing occurrence.

"Be sure to bring the man's umbrella on Wednesday," he added.

This note he dispatched with his secretary to the lady's London home.

Her reply arrived in record time. It expressed consternation that anybody should know about her experience with the masher; in fact, the lady had made up her mind that no one ever would know.

"I will bring the broken umbrella, but it was my umbrella, not his," she amplified. Stead afterwards stated that this was the only discrepancy in the amusing and amazing psychically received message.

Although he always had taken an interest in psychic research, it had begun really to dominate his personal life a few years before. Shortly after founding the *Review of Reviews,* he had written to F. W. H. Meyers, declaring that in the Proceedings of the Society for Psychic Research there was indeed a bonanza of newsworthy material. If properly employed, he knew it would yield him a Christmas issue full of "authentic apparitions to astound all readers." In his letter to Meyers he added that he would be delighted to avail himself of any assistance they could give him.

"To present a ghost to my public is a difficult task which I must not depute to another, however abler and more competent he may be from the scientific point of view." This from the man who, when editor of the *Pall Mall Gazette,* had introduced modern journalism as we know it today, including the interview and the personality profile, the man whose editorial campaigns against vice had landed him in prison for "dealing in pornographic journalism"!

The more Stead practiced automatic writing the more amazing he found the results. The strange gift he had so suddenly discovered brought messages from friends living at a distance, as well as from persons long dead. Many persons laughed at him, but thousands of others realized that W. T. Stead possessed strange powers.

In 1892 he visited his close friend and associate, Lady Henry Somerset, at Eastnor Castle, the family seat of the Somersets. There he met a young American woman to whom he refers simply as "Miss E." Two years before, and quite by coincidence, he had met her closest friend, Miss Julia Ames, also an American girl. "Miss E" now told him Julia had died soon after they had made a pact that the first one to die would appear to the other, in order to prove the "reality of the world beyond the grave." Knowing Stead's absorbing interest in spiritualism, "Miss E" told him how Julia had appeared to her in Chicago, rousing her from sleep. She appeared to be "radiantly happy," but had remained silent before vanishing. The second time Julia's spirit appeared was at Eastnor Castle. This time "Miss E" was wide awake and saw her friend appear "as distinct and as real as in life." Again no spoken word passed between them. Now that "Miss E" was again visiting at Eastnor, she hoped Stead would try to contact the dead Julia.

The next morning before breakfast, in his own room, Stead's hand wrote a message that was "brief and to the point." Its text was, "Tell her to remember what I said when last we came to Minerva." Stead protested that this message was silly, but his pen wrote insistently that "Miss E" would understand.

"I felt so chagrined at the absurdity of the message," Stead says, "that for a long time I refused to deliver it."

When he finally did relay the message, "Miss E" exclaimed that it couldn't have come from anyone but Julia.

But how, Stead demanded, could she "come to Minerva?" It just did not make sense.

"Miss E" explained that shortly before death, Julia had facetiously applied the name of the ancient goddess to Miss Frances Elizabeth Willard, the founder of the Women's Christian Temperance Union. She had even presented Miss Willard with a "Minerva" cameo brooch. The two young women had called her by that nickname to the exclusion of all other names. The message received by Stead was substantially identical with one given by Julia the last time "Miss E" and "Minerva" had visited her when she was on her death-bed.

"Here again," Stead points out, "there was a slight mistake. Minerva had come to Julia, instead of Julia going to Minerva, but otherwise, the message was correct."

This first message touched off a series of automatically written communications from Julia. Wherever psychic research is of interest, this collection of the "Julia Letters" is believed to be unshakable proof that there is life beyond the tomb.

One of the most interesting and most meaningful of the "Julia Letters" to come to Stead automatically, is dated August 11, 1893:

"I want to tell you more about the experiences I had when I passed over ... I will tell you how I felt when I first saw my body lying in bed. I ought to have told you that when I found myself standing by the bedside, I was completely dressed. I did not recognize myself as being anything different from what I had always been. I felt just the same. I had on the same kind of clothes and was, so far as I could see, just the same—nothing altered ... The first thing that made me see that I was different was discovering my old body lying on the bed. It seemed so strange to see myself lying quite still and to know that I was not myself but only the cast-off chrysalis of my real self. When I looked at it as it lay there, I felt somewhat sorry, for I had been in the old thing for thirty years or more, and when you have worn a dress or a body so long, you kind of feel attached to it. And there it lay, quiet and silent and senseless, and I looked at it and wondered what would happen, now that I was outside of it. I was just a bit frightened, but I was consoled because everything seemed so familiar. It was just the same as it always was. But it was not till the door opened and Miss Willard entered and begin to cry over my old body that I really began to realize that I was really what you call dead, and yet I was never more alive in my whole existence."

After the first "Minerva" message, Stead and "Miss E" decided to try for further communications. This time they sat at opposite ends of a long table. After his hand had written answers to various questions, Stead asked Julia if, as a further test, she would use his hand to recall to her friend's memory some incident in their lives of which he himself had no knowledge.

His hand wrote: "Ask her if she can remember when we were going home together, when she fell and hurt her spine."

"That fills the bill!" Stead laughed triumphantly. "I never knew you had met with such an accident!"

But "Miss E" was completely bewildered, and protested to Julia that never in her existence had she injured her spine in any way.

Nevertheless, Stead's hand continued: "I am quite right. She has forgotten." The entity explained how, seven years before, at Streator, Ill., when the young women were returning home from their office on a Saturday afternoon, "Miss E" slipped on the snow-glazed curbstone "opposite Mrs. Bull's house."

"Miss E" was overwhelmed. Now she recalled the mishap, and remembered that the resultant bad back had kept her in bed for days.

In 1897 Stead's first volume of the collected letters was issued. This work was entitled *Letters from Julia*, and subtitled *Light from the Borderline— received by automatic writing from one who has gone before*. In twelve years it enjoyed seven printings, and was translated into French, German, Italian, Russian, and Hindustani. There were also editions in the Scandinavian languages and Greek.

Stead crossed the Atlantic for the first time in October, 1893, becoming the most talked-about foreign visitor in years. In Chicago he became enmeshed in deep trouble when, in addressing a ladies' club, he stated "the obvious fact that the idle and worthless rich" are infinitely more disreputable than the most depraved women.

A month later, he was interviewed by the *Chicago Sunday Tribune* about his forthcoming newspaper, the *Daily Paper*. The interview was as astonishing as it was passionately honest. When asked about his activities in psychic research, Stead said: "That reminds me that I must tell you about a remarkable feature in my newspaper ... It is publishing for the first time in the world's history an interview between two persons who were separated from each other by a distance of eight hundred miles, who had no wire or material means of communication ... In my sample paper I shall publish an interview with Lady Brooke ... on the future of the British aristocracy. When that interview took place, I was in a railway carriage at Dover and Lady Brooke was with her sister, the Duchess of Sutherland, at Dunrobin Castle, in the extreme north of Scotland. I interviewed Lady Brooke by my automatic, telepathic hand, without having to go to the trouble of telegraphing to her, or writing to her, or asking for the privilege."

"How on earth did you accomplish this?"

"I simply took a pencil in my hand, spread a sheet of blank paper on a blotting pad in the railway carriage, and in thought addressed to Lady Brooke the questions that I should have asked her if she had been sitting on the opposite side of the carriage. Then my hand, without more ado, wrote out her answer to each question. Then I asked another question, and she answered it, and so on, just as if the two parties had been face to face in the ordinary journalistic fashion. When the interview was finished, I put it in my pocket, and on arriving in London an hour later, I found a letter from Lady Brooke addressed to me, which had arrived that morning. When I opened it, I found it contained, in brief, the substance of the remarks which she had made to me, writing through my hand. When I sent a proof of the interview down to her, she returned it without correction or erasure, stating that it was marvelous—the perfect accuracy with which I had tapped her mind and had succeeded in procuring a written record of her thoughts. The only criticism she had to make was that she wished I had added something more—an amplification of what she had already said. This also corresponded with my own impression, having got so sleepy from fatigue in travel from Switzerland all night that I didn't go on with it."

In the early spring of 1912, Stead wrote in his magazine about an invitation he had received to speak in America. "The committee has been kind enough to ask me to address a meeting held under their auspices on World's Peace in Carnegie Hall, New York, on April 21st, at which President Taft and others will be among the speakers. I expect to leave by the Titanic on April 10th..."

Stead left home, radiating enthusiasm at the size and magnificence of the Titanic. Mrs. Stead later recalled him as he stood on deck, waving to her as the giant ship steamed off on what was to be her first and last voyage. Mrs. William Shelley, a fellow passenger who survived the wreck of the Titanic, gives us this eye-witness account of Stead's last hours:

"He was one of the very few who were actually on deck when the iceberg was struck. I saw him soon after and was thoroughly scared, but he preserved the most beautiful composure. Whether he stayed on board or sought safety by leaping into the sea I cannot tell, but I do know he faced death with philosophic calm."

In 1914 Stead's collected "Julia Letters" came out in a new, enlarged edition and were entitled *After Death: A Personal Interview*. The Preface had been written by Stead in 1909 and was originally intended by him for inclusion in a second volume which never was realized. However, the later "Julia Letters," which Stead did not have the opportunity to edit and revise, were considered to be of such inestimable value that his daughter included them in the new edition exactly as her father had received them.

In the Preface, Stead voices not only his personal views which were the result of a lifetime of probing, but also the views of people everywhere who seek the truth:

"I am addressing myself solely to those who are willing to admit that there is at least an 'off chance' that all the religions and most of the philosophies—to say nothing of the universal instinct of the human race— may have had some foundation for the conviction that there is a life after death. Put the percentage of possibility as low as you like; if there be even the smallest chance of its truth, it is surely an obvious corollary from such an admission that there is no subject more worthy of careful and scientific examination."

Always the hard-boiled newspaperman who wanted above all to face facts, Stead was also the rebel with a cause on behalf of the downtrodden, the exploited, the misunderstood. Frederick Whyte, his distinguished biographer, sums up Stead's absorption with psychic research thus:

"Whatever view we take of this phase of William Stead's life, it would be foolish to attempt to divorce it from his general career—to treat it as an aberration from the main current of his character ... He was a spirit who refused to remain in the prison of his senses. The passion to penetrate the mysteries of the unseen sprang from the same qualities as those which made him the incomparable journalist he was."

AUNT CAROLINE'S TRYST with DEATH

Peggy Maurine Gregson

When I was ten years old I went on a visit to a big cotton plantation in Helena, Ark., to spend a month with Great Aunt Caroline. I recall clearly how depressing I found the atmosphere of the once-gorgeous mansion; how silent I found the rooms which a generation ago had rung with the laughter of beautifully gowned people on my aunt's wedding night. As I wandered through the lonely house I thought many times of the story I had heard of the way they had danced there in the big front hall under the glittering chandeliers, had toasted the bride and groom, and had listened to the strains of the old waltzes mingled with the night noises drifting in on the rose- and wisteria-scented air.

Then the young Confederate bridegroom dressed in gray had marched away to war. He never returned. And the house had become very quiet, and Aunt Caroline had grown old in the quietness.

On one of the days of my visit there, in 1919, I was forbidden to go out of doors to play so I roamed through the dark rooms and finally found myself in the attic. There I came across an old box filled with faded letters, invitations, diaries, and keepsakes. Looking through them I read the story of Aunt Caroline Palmer Lee's life. In one yellowed envelope I found a pink rose which crumbled when I touched it. And I remembered that downstairs in the hall hung a portrait of my aunt in her wedding dress. In the portrait she wore a pink rose in her hair. I wondered if I had found the original rose.

During my visit there were other sunnier days, and that summer I often climbed up into the hills behind the house to sit and dream. As I have said, I found the mansion at 404 College Street depressing. It stood in the shadow of the great magnolia trees outside; inside were the shadows of bygone splendor and a long-ago love.

One day as I walked slowly on the hills beyond the cotton fields I stumbled across an old graveyard where, apparently unknown, fallen Confederate soldiers had been buried. The graves were shallow and had been washed by the rains of many, many springs. The tombstones still standing by some of the graves were moss covered and crumbling.

As I stood idly kicking the toe of my shoe in one of the graves I unearthed a piece of old musket and some sort of round object. I scraped the dirt from the small round thing and held half of an old-fashioned locket in my hand. Under its glass was the picture of a beautiful girl. I caught my breath, remembering that the other half of just such a locket hung around Aunt Caroline's neck. Her half-a-locket contained the picture of a young soldier.

Even after all these years I can still feel the suffocating beat of my heart as I looked at that half of a locket in my hand. Then I glanced up and saw my aunt running up the hill toward me.

Although I recognized Aunt Caroline, she wasn't old! She was young, beautiful, and on her face was an eager smile. She held her lacy, billowing skirts in a small white hand and just the tips of her satin shoes showed as she rushed past me to grasp the hand of a young Confederate soldier who now stood beside the grave where I had found the locket. The soldier was dressed in a gray battle uniform, handsome and smiling. They turned away from me and, hand in hand, disappeared.

Several minutes later I had started to descend the hill toward home when I saw Tom, who had been with Aunt Caroline for half a century, hurrying towards me with his tottering gait.

"Miss Peggy!" he gasped. "Miss Caroline! She done passed on now!"

Later, at Aunt Caroline's funeral, while the others wept I could not cry. I knew she had been happy to go, back to a love which had lasted all the lonely years of her life and which she had taken with her straight through the gates of Paradise.

I HAUNTED AN ORCHARD

Margaret C. Wilson

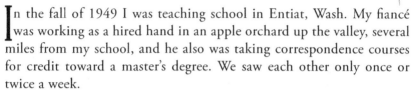

In the fall of 1949 I was teaching school in Entiat, Wash. My fiancé was working as a hired hand in an apple orchard up the valley, several miles from my school, and he also was taking correspondence courses for credit toward a master's degree. We saw each other only once or twice a week.

The weather had turned cold before the apple harvest was completed and everyone worked long hours to save the crop which made most of the region's living. Ray worked extra too, in addition to his studies, and he seemed tired and on edge one evening when he called for me for our regular Saturday date.

In no mood even for a movie, Ray drove the car aimlessly for a while before he remarked, "Maggie, who were you out with last Monday?"

I was surprised. "Why, Ray, I wasn't out with anybody. I was home, correcting papers!"

"No, you weren't. Johnny saw you in town with somebody." (Johnny was a friend of Ray's.)

I denied being with anybody else; it was not true, but Ray's jealous temper was aroused and nothing I could say convinced him. Finally I lost my temper and we quarreled heatedly. It was still early when he left me at my door without even a "good night."

Alone in my apartment, my anger gradually cooled. Why couldn't he realize I loved him and would not even look at another man? I cried myself to sleep.

And then I dreamed I was in an apple orchard, walking up and down beneath the trees. I was weeping aloud, with all the heartache and loneliness of the ages heaped upon me, it seemed. The night was cold, but the coldness I felt was spiritual. I was alone in the universe. The night was completely black, but somehow I saw the trees as silver forms, complete in every detail of shadowless bark and leafless branch. The closeness of the trees comforted me.

The noise of my alarm clock jarred me awake, but it was difficult to arouse myself from lethargy. The dream had seemed like reality; daylight

17

seemed a dream.

Weeks passed. When harvest was over Ray got a job as a dishwasher in a hotel in the sleepy town that is Wenatchee in winter. Our dates continued. We had made up our quarrel but something was missing.

I no longer remember what started our next quarrel, but it was worse than the first. I had tried to be on guard against anything that might lead to another quarrel, and self-recrimination added to my misery as I went to bed that night.

Again, the apple orchard shone silver against the darkness and the cold of my dream. I walked up and down, disconsolate and alone. Love was far away and dead. The bare branches bent over me in silent sympathy.

Then the alarm jolted me awake to the workaday world.

I dreamed often that winter, and not always after a quarrel. The dream was always the same: the orchard with its silver trees, the cold, the loneliness. And always afterward I adjusted to the objective world again with difficulty.

One night, toward spring, the dream was different. I was walking up and down as usual, when I saw a man standing by a tree. He seemed like a shadow, dark against the silver tree, but his eyes held a light of their own; brilliant, hard, they held me and drew me to him.

I heard his voice, deep and vibrant, "In the name of the Father, the Son and the Holy Ghost, I command you, spirit, get you gone from this orchard and never come back."

With a violent wrench the breath seemed torn from me and I awoke in my own bed. The night was still dark around me; it was between midnight and dawn.

After that I had no more dreams.

Ray and I were drifting apart, but still I clung to him, even though he made my life miserable with his unreasoning jealousy.

Although I dreamed no more, now I had a violent headache which never left me. My work began to suffer.

I became increasingly irritable with my students and they retaliated by becoming noisy and hard to manage.

One day the Principal called me into his office, "Margaret, you've got to pull yourself together. You've done a good job in your classes until just lately. You've let down, and a teacher can't afford to let herself go. If you're having trouble of some sort I'll help if I can, but you can't keep on like this or I'll have to ask you to resign."

I wanted to complain of my headache, but realized that he would just send me to a doctor. I felt my problems were psychological and that straightening things out with Ray would clear them up.

That evening, however, I decided I needed professional help; if I had not been able to straighten things out with Ray in all these months I certainly could not do it now, with extra anxiety for my job on my mind.

So on a Saturday in April I sat in the outer office of the only psychologist in Wenatchee. When the receptionist beckoned me into the inner office I was greeted by a pleasant looking middle-aged man. There was something faintly familiar in his voice as he began questioning me about my troubles. As I talked he listened, frowning slightly. I found myself telling him about my recurring dreams.

His face brightened with interest. "Are you sure it was always the same orchard?"

I nodded.

"Do you have these dreams still?" he asked.

"No," I replied, and described my final dream and the man who had ordered me away from the orchard.

"It can't be possible! I don't believe it!" He rose abruptly and turned to stare out the window. I saw he was tense and excited.

I bridled. "Do you doubt me?"

He turned back to the desk with a wry smile. "No, I don't doubt you, but I almost doubt myself."

"Whatever do you mean?"

"Have you heard of 'astral projection'?" he asked. I nodded and he continued, "Last fall a woman came to me, highly disturbed, and said she was afraid she was losing her mind. Her husband owns a large apple orchard near where you teach. It seems the orchard was being haunted by a very noisy ghost. She was frightened and thought she was hearing things. The worst of it was, it didn't occur every night, or even regularly—just when she was especially upset over something. Two or three weeks would go by and everything would be quiet; then in the night, shortly before midnight, an unearthly sobbing would begin and continue until dawn.

"The woman was perfectly healthy; I was able to help her with some of her problems, but the sobbing in the orchard continued. Finally she insisted that I spend some time with her and her family to see if I could hear it, too. I didn't like the idea—but it was the only thing that would satisfy her. I was there every night for two solid weeks before the noises occurred. Then I understood what she was talking about. It was enough to unnerve anyone.

"I've been interested in psychic phenomena for years and never doubted that it was a real ghost. But now, it seems, I was wrong. I exorcised you—or your astral self—from that orchard. Your headache results from your avenue of escape being cut off. Does this sound reasonable to you?"

I thought a minute, then nodded. Astral projection would explain why my dreams had seemed so real and why it had been so hard to awaken afterward.

After talks with this doctor my headache receded, and after several months I was able to let Ray go. When we finally broke up my headache left completely and it hasn't returned.

Nor have I dreamed since.

DO WE HAVE THE RIGHT "TIME"?

Alson J. Smith

"Time," cried a perplexed Saint Augustine, "...what is it? If nobody asks me, I know. But if I am asked, I do not know!"

What is time? Is our concept of it as an absolute the correct one? Through the centuries a large and impressive body of evidence has accumulated to indicate that time is not an absolute, and that our conception of it is as naive as Aristotle's firm belief that the earth was flat and the stars fixed.

Precognitions have appeared regularly in the literature not only of psychical research but of science itself for more than two thousand years. The Bible is full of them. The London Society for Psychical Research has compiled a file of more than one thousand proven premonitory dreams. They pop up in the daily papers quite monotonously.

For instance: on a Friday evening in late July, 1958, seventeen-year-old Betty J. March, of Boston, casually told her mother that on the following morning she and her boyfriend, Paul Zanet, twenty-four, were going to drive up into the White Mountains for a day's outing, returning to Boston that night. Zanet was a graduate student at M.I.T., a mature and capable young man, and the day's drive to the mountains and back was one that thousands of Bostonians take every summer. The weather was pleasant and Mrs. March was not at all concerned.

When Mrs. March retired on Saturday night the young people had not yet returned. She was still not concerned, but no sooner had she dropped off to sleep than she had a vivid dream. In the dream she "saw" her daughter, dressed in black pedal-pushers, a white sweatshirt, and tennis shoes, and Zanet attired in khaki shirt and pants and also wearing tennis shoes, lying on a high mountain ledge. Rain mixed with sleet drove in on the huddled figures; the wind screamed and howled. A voice said, "They are dead." Then Mrs. March woke up.

Thoroughly frightened, she called the Boston police and told them about the dream. They alerted the New Hampshire state police, and early Sunday morning they discovered Zanet's car parked near the base of 6,288-foot Mount Washington, the highest peak in New England.

Although the weather at the foot of Mount Washington and in New

England generally had been good on Saturday, it had been a different story near the peak, where the temperature had dropped to thirty-nine degrees and a cold, driving rain mixed with sleet had been driven by seventy-five-mile-an-hour winds.

Searchers found the bodies of the couple huddled together under a ledge about a quarter of a mile from the summit. They had died of exhaustion and exposure. Betty was wearing black pedal-pushers and a white sweatshirt, and Zanet wore a khaki shirt and trousers. Both had on tennis shoes.

It was all as Mrs. March had seen it in her dream. At the exact time of the dream, the medical report showed, the young people had still been alive, so precognition and not clairvoyance was involved.

Is there such a thing as precognition? The parapsychologists tell us that apparently there is, for laboratory experiments under rigid test conditions at Duke and elsewhere give odds of 400,000 to one against chance being responsible for the positive results obtained. There is a power or capacity of the mind that is not limited by space or time. The implications of this discovery are staggering, the principal one being that our concept of time is erroneous, or at best incomplete.

There seem to be four identifiable types of general precognitions: trivial, beneficial, non-beneficial, and detrimental.

A trivial precognition is one which may take place only a few minutes or seconds before the actual occurrence of the rather unimportant event previsioned. For instance, F.W.H. Myers tells about a certain Mrs. C. who had a vivid dream of being chased by a monkey. Mrs. C. had always disliked monkeys, to be sure, but the dream appeared ridiculous because there are very few monkeys in England where Mrs. C. lived. However, the dream disturbed her and she recounted it to her husband. He suggested that she was just nervous and, since it was a pleasant afternoon, might profit by taking their two children for a brisk walk. This she did, taking them down a lane which ran along the side of a high stone wall shielding the residence of the Duke of Argyll.

As they passed the Duke's coach-house Mrs. C. was amazed to see a monkey appear suddenly on the roof—the exact monkey of her dream. In fear and wonder she cried out, "My dream! My dream!" The monkey, hearing her, jumped from the roof to the wall and began chasing the fleeing Mrs. C. and the two children. A coachman, hearing the commotion, ran out of the coach-house and captured the monkey.

The monkey—certainly a rarity in England—was a very valuable one kept by the Duchess of Argyll as a pet. It had gotten loose and jumped to the coach-house roof a few seconds before Mrs. C. and the children appeared.

A beneficial precognition is one that does the recipient some good. Mr. Wade Stevick, a businessman of Southern Pines, N. C., had a rather vague premonition that something was about to happen that would take him away from his business for an extended period.

He says:

"The previous day I had made several collections, but for some reason I had kept in my safe that day much more money than ever before. I usually paid all bills by check. I had finished to a quite unusual degree all carpenter and repair work, procured ample necessities, and, to make a summation, there was not one detail left undone which would have caused someone else to do anything unusual in connection with my business while I was away.

"About 7:30 p.m. Saturday, December 30, a telegram revealed that my mother, at her home in Ohio, had dropped unconscious (never revived) from a cerebral hemorrhage. This caused me to be away from my business until January 10." (*Journal of the American Society For Psychical Research*, Vol. L, Nos. 2-3, 1956)

Although the event dimly previsioned was tragic, the precognition was beneficial in that it enabled Mr. Stevick to put his business in order ahead of time.

In the third category of precognition, non-beneficial, the future is "seen" quite clearly, but the previsioning does not result in any change of events to the benefit of the one doing the previsioning. An excellent illustration of this non-beneficial type is the following:

In early July, 1750, the sloop *Liverpool* docked at Oxford, Md., with a cargo consigned to Mr. Robert Morris, the father of the great Revolutionary financier. It was customary in those days for the consignee to go aboard a ship carrying his cargo and be entertained by the captain, after which he would receive a salute from one of the ship's guns. Mr. Morris, however, had had a dream in which he "saw" himself having dinner with the captain and then being fatally wounded by the salute fired in his honor as he left the ship. He apologized to the captain, told him about the strange dream, and asked to be excused from the dinner. The captain demurred and promised that in view of the dream no salute would be fired, so Mr. Morris reluctantly agreed to go aboard.

When it was time for Mr. Morris to leave the ship, the captain asked if he would not change his mind about the salute. "You know, a glass of grog is served to every sailor immediately after a salute," he said, "so the crew don't take kindly to the arrangement."

They argued about it for a while, but finally Morris agreed to let the salute be fired provided that it should be done when the boat taking him ashore was a safe distance away from the *Liverpool,* and that either the captain, who was going ashore with him, or he himself, gave the signal to fire. The captain agreed.

The captain and Mr. Morris pulled away in a small rowboat. But before they were out of range, a fly settled on the captain's nose. He raised his hand to brush it off and the gunner, thinking he was giving the agreed signal, fired the salute. The ball splashed harmlessly into the water well away from the row-boat, but the wadding from the gun struck Morris on the arm, breaking the bone. Blood-poisoning set in, and on July 12, 1750, he died!

In this case the precognition was distinctly non-beneficial, and may even belong in the detrimental category.

In detrimental precognition, the precognition seems actually to help produce the result, usually undesirable, that is foreseen. For instance, in the 1957 Kentucky Derby the odds-on favorite was a horse named Gallant Man. Gallant Man was owned by Mr. Ralph Lowe and was to be ridden by one of the country's top jockeys, Willie Shoemaker.

On the night before the race Mr. Lowe had a strange dream. In it he "saw" Gallant Man leading, coming down the stretch, only to be pulled up short of the finish line by the jockey while another horse shot past to win. The next morning he warned Willie Shoemaker: "Don't pull him up short, Willie!" Willie gave him a queer look; never in the entire history of the Kentucky Derby had a horse been pulled up short of the finish line.

When the race was run the next afternoon, Gallant Man had a comfortable lead coming into the home stretch.

Then, as the horses pounded towards the finish line, the crowd was amazed to see Willie Shoemaker mistake the 16th pole for the finish line and pull up Gallant Man. Iron Liege thundered past to win by half a length.

Mr. Lowe's precognition was detrimental in that it helped to bring about the result previsioned, since the idea of pulling the horse up short would probably not have entered Willie Shoemaker's mind at all if Mr. Lowe had not mentioned the possibility.

These are the general precognitions.

There is also a category in which the previsioning is vague, not entering into the consciousness at all. This is called subliminal precognition. A hunch, for instance, is a kind of subliminal precognition.

Mr. W.E. Cox of Southern Pines, N.C., has conducted an extremely interesting study of subliminal or hunch previsioning based on railroad accident rates. The chief sources for the study were the Interstate Commerce Commission's annual lists of all accidents on Class One railroads. Mr. Cox limited his study to the thirty-five railroads which had one or more accidents in the periods between 1950 and 1955, supplementing his analyses of the ICC lists with personal correspondence with the vice-presidents or traffic managers of the thirty-five roads. His method was to compare the passenger-loads, both coach and Pullman, at a certain checkpoint on the day when an accident occurred on a particular train with its normal load on that day, and the passenger-load for the week during which an accident occurred with its normal load for that week. Making due allowance for the operation of chance, Cox established mathematically the amazing fact that in a large majority of the accidents the passenger-load for that day and that week was either the lowest or next to the lowest of all the days and weeks studied! He concluded that the only explanation for this consistently lower number of train-riders on accident days or weeks was subliminal precognition—in other words, many people who would normally have taken the train on the day or during the week of an accident had a hunch that something was going to happen and stayed off the trains during that time.

Just as the mind apparently has the ability to look forward in time, so it seems to have the ability to look backward. Retrocognition has also been the subject of laboratory testing at Duke and elsewhere, and while it has not been established statistically as firmly as has precognition, nevertheless the tests have strongly supported its existence. A good illustration of retrocognition is to be found in a little book called *An Adventure,* which was first published in 1911 and has been republished as recently as 1947. It was written by two estimable English ladies who were also distinguished scholars. C. Anne E. Moberly, principal of St. Hugh's College, Oxford, and Eleanor F. Jourdain, a member of her staff who later succeeded her at St. Hugh's.

The two Englishwomen, traveling in France, visited the Petit Trianon at Versailles in August, 1901. The Petit Trianon, however, was quite different from what they had expected. The air was still and oppressive, and both women later confessed that, without saying anything about it to the other, each had felt like screaming with nervousness. There were no other tourists about. The buildings did not seem to be where current maps located them, and some were not on the maps at all. The gardeners and others whom they encountered were dressed in the clothes of another era and spoke archaic French. They saw strange-looking people and heard strange noises. A pretty woman, dressed in a long-outmoded cape, sketched in a garden, and an evil-looking man with a pockmarked face followed them about. Everything was odd, eerie, and old. The two teachers finally retired from the Petit Trianon, baffled but relieved to be out of the strange atmosphere.

Later they returned to the Petit Trianon and discovered it to be quite different than it had appeared on their first visit. There were crowds of tourists about; gardeners, attendants and gendarmes were dressed as they should be; and everything was in the right place as shown on the maps. The Petit Trianon they had seen the first time had disappeared!

There then began for the two scholarly Englishwomen a long process of comparing old maps, documents, and fashion books, and an exhaustive correspondence with French historians and other authorities. Their research finally convinced the ladies that the Petit Trianon they had "seen" on the occasion of their first visit was not the present day Petit Trianon but the Petit Trianon as it had been at the time of Marie Antoinette—1789! The documents they offered in substantiation of this theory were taken seriously enough to be accepted by the Bodleian Library.

If precognition and retrocognition are facts, then time is not the absolute we have assumed it to be. Maurice Maeterlinck, the playwright, speaks of a "plurality of times which are merely pure conventions" and questions our smug assumption that there is only a single dimension of time—the one we know. Immanuel Kant observed that our conception of time might be due to the special pattern in which our sensory apparatus has evolved; the true order of the universe, he thought, might be quite otherwise. And there have been fictional questionings of our time-concept, like Edward Bellamy's *Looking Backwards,* and H.G. Wells' *The Time Machine,* to say nothing of today's science fiction writers.

One theory of time which would accommodate precognition and retrocognition is the one advanced by the late J.W. Dunne, a British engineer. After a long study of precognitive dreams Dunne developed a theory of serialism, which holds that reality as it appears to science has to be a series of regresses reaching back into infinity.

The time-barrier, according to Dunne's theory, is really nonexistent and is merely the creation of consciousness, and there is a faculty of the subconscious which pays no attention to the alleged barrier.

Another interesting theory is advanced by Dr. C.D. Broad, an English scientist. Dr. Broad believes that there may be a second dimension of time lying at right angles to our familiar dimension, and that something which is future in our familiar dimension may be past in this second, unfamiliar dimension.

Still another time-speculation is based on the idea, generally accepted in psychology, that the "present moment" in which we act is not a mere point-instant, but occupies a definite period of duration. Within this "spacious present" there is no present, past, or future, but rather a graduation with respect to clearness of apprehension of whatever lies within its compass, maximum clearness being at the exact center.

Do we have the right "time"?

Probably not. The great pioneering of the twenty-first century may well be done on this time-frontier. Here man may discover the greatest of his natural resources.

Time! What is it? We do not really know. But tomorrow we may begin to know.

THE DEAD HAVE VOICES

Louis Whitsitt

The mysterious disappearance of eleven-year-old Matilda Russo, of Moorestown, N.J., in 1921, from in front of her home less than five minutes after she answered her mother's call to supper, had supernatural overtones from the outset. Ellis Parker entered the case shortly after Matilda vanished. The Burlington County crime-buster ordered his men to search every neighboring house. Not a single building, cellar, or attic was overlooked. But the girl's disappearance still remained a riddle.

Parker questioned Louis Lively, a man of excellent reputation, two hours after entering the case. As the nearest neighbor to the Russo family, he might have been expected to feel some decent sympathy in the matter, yet the sleuth found him to be uncooperative and downright discourteous. Parker was incensed at Lively when he growled, "No use snoopin' around my place. The kid ain't here."

Twice, while Lively was away working, Parker searched his home. A dirt floor in Lively's basement suggested to the detective that Lively, while his wife was away, had lured little Matilda into the house, murdered her, then buried her body in the cellar. A pile of refuse, covered with cobwebs, lay in the center of the floor. Parker's imagination stirred. Although unbroken cobwebs clearly indicated that the refuse beneath had long been undisturbed, he started an inch-by-inch probe of the balance of the dirt floor. Such probing proved fruitless.

Three nights after Matilda vanished Parker was called to the telephone in his Mt. Holly home. "Detective Parker?" an anguished woman's voice asked. "Can you come right over? I just heard my little girl's voice through an open window. I'm certain she is being held in Louis Lively's house!"

Parker hastened to Moorestown. "It wasn't my imagination," cried the unnerved mother. "I awakened from a sound sleep to hear Matilda crying, 'Mother.'"

Parker tried to comfort Mrs. Russo. "Now, leave everything to me. We are going to find Matilda. But we won't disturb Louis Lively tonight. Tomorrow when he goes to work I'll turn his place upside down," he promised, looking into the honest, intelligent face of the grief-stricken mother. Parker frankly believed the girl to be dead; and he did not believe in ghosts!

An extensive search took Parker and his men from attic to basement in the Lively house. Again they studied the refuse pile, then Parker said aloud, "But if he buried her there the cobwebs would have been disturbed. Nope, she's not down here."

It happened again the next night.

Mrs. Russo was ironing clothes in her kitchen. The roof faced a side of Lively's darkened house. Her daughter's voice again cried out to her. "Mother! Mother!" Matilda screamed in mortal terror.

It was dark outside. Mrs. Russo dropped her work, rushed outdoors, and circled the house without hearing anything more. Fear clutched her heart as she hastened inside to telephone the detective again.

"I know my little girl is in that terrible man's house," she insisted. "She just called to me again."

Lively wasn't home when Parker reached his house. Almost certain in his mind that Mrs. Russo had suffered a serious mental aberration, he figured there was only one place left to search. Heading straight for the basement, he grabbed a crowbar and started probing the rubbish pile. Soft earth quickly exposed the suspect's fiendish crime. Little Matilda Russo was found.

Explaining the crime's solution, the hard-boiled rural detective, who previously refused to believe in the supernatural, said, "That little girl called her mother through God!"

Such cases as this make it appear that a plausible answer to the riddle of clairvoyance would be well worth all its cost in effort and money.

Tomorrow may be the day an enigmatic message from an undetermined source will change the pattern of your life.

THE EXORCISM OF THE FIVE DEVILS OF ANNA ECKLUND

James L. Waring

In the convent of the Franciscan Sisters, at Earling, Iowa, the solemn ceremony of exorcism was about to begin.

The possessed woman, forty-year-old Anna Ecklund, lay fully clothed on the bare mattress of a large, old-fashioned iron bed. Her dress was tightly secured as a precaution against improper diabolical tricks—a measure suggested by some singular events of the preceding day.

On the train trip to Earling the woman had fought like a she-devil. The train crew—forewarned that she was subject to "fits"—got her to her destination with difficulty.

Father Joseph Steiger, parish priest of Earling, had a lot of inexplicable trouble with his brand-new car and was two hours late getting to the station to meet Mrs. Ecklund and the Rev. Theophilus Riesinger, O.M. CAP., the exorcist.

Now, tiny drops of perspiration beaded Anna Ecklund's forehead, though the Iowa morning was cool. It was September 1, 1928.

There was a light knock on Anna Ecklund's door. A young Sister, barely out of novitiate, entered the room, smiling nervously. "Mrs. Ecklund, our morning Mass was specially offered for your intention. They're ready now. We'll all pray very hard for you."

The Mother Superior entered, followed by a corps of Sisters. Two of them had been registered nurses before entering the religious life. All of them were strong, disciplined women. They fingered their long fifteen-decade Franciscan rosaries and took prearranged positions around Anna's bed.

Next Father Joseph Steiger entered. He was to witness the incredible affair from beginning to end. It had been necessary to get his permission, as well as that of the Mother Superior, before the woman could be brought into the parish, or the convent, for such a rite. The Bishop, as well as the exorcist, had warned Father Steiger solemnly of the possible consequences.

"The devil," Father Riesinger had said, "doesn't take this sort of interference lying down. The point is," went on the Capuchin, a life-long friend of the pastor, "your parish seems the most suitable. Neither the woman, nor her family, could bear it in her home. It's quiet here, and far enough from where she lives that she won't have to spend the rest of her life being pointed at as "the woman who had a devil."

Father Steiger, perhaps understandably, hedged. "I know we've gone over this before—but, Father Theo, this is twentieth-century Iowa!"

"And the woman's case of possession is genuine," Father Theophilus Riesinger said. "The Church moves too slowly for there to be any mistake. She's been suffering since she was fourteen. Add it up for yourself. A good and pious girl gets obsessed with the most unbelievable lusts—so distasteful to her she wants to hang herself. She wants to go to the Sacraments—and voices mock her, make her life hell. Year after year, every priest she goes to gives her the same advice: 'Go see a good doctor.' She's been to more than a dozen—the best in Milwaukee and Chicago—and what do they say? There's nothing wrong with her—nothing at all! She gets married and her condition gets worse—far worse. The last time she forced herself to go to confession, for example, she got an urge to strangle the confessor. Then, of course, there's the business of tongues."

Anna Ecklund, the girl who never got past the eighth grade, did not *speak* in tongues. She understood them. When her distraught husband begged the parish priest to drive out and bless their home, Anna kept screaming a literal translation of the Latin prayers. She presented a frightening picture of a woman who knew exactly what she was doing, yet was unable to stop.

Faced with what the Church regards as a final, unmistakable sign of diabolic possession, the Bishop reexamined the case—first presented to his office back in 1902, and added to by every priest sent to Anna's parish over the intervening years—and decided he had to act.

Finally he put the affair of Anna Ecklund in the care of a Capuchin already noted for his success in a dozen cases of possession. This Capuchin was the last person to enter Anna Ecklund's room on that morning of September 1, 1928.

Father Theophilus Riesinger, nearing sixty, was still a strong, muscular man, in excellent physical condition from a lifetime of disciplined monastic living. With his venerable beard and crucifix tucked like a short-sword through the cincture of his Capuchin robes, he looked like some patriarch from the past. Compared to the others that morning, he was relaxed, almost calm.

Every candidate ordained to the priesthood receives, among other

Orders, the Minor Order of Exorcist—"the power to place your hands upon those possessed and through the imposition of the hands, the grace of the Holy Ghost, and the words of exorcism, you shall drive evil spirits out of the bodies of those possessed."

Though common in the early days of Christianity, it's almost a forgotten rite today—unfamiliar even to many Catholics. Few priests ever use it and, nowadays, never without the full approval of superiors. Because of the sacrament of Baptism, a primary tenet of all Christian religions, and other rites, the Church feels that cases of true diabolic possession are exceedingly rare. Moreover, it's a matter of policy that such cases are not made public.

The case of Anna Ecklund is the exception.

"In the Name of the Father and of the Son and of the Holy Ghost!"

The venerable Capuchin made the Sign of the Cross. The woman on the bed began to tremble as those present joined in the opening prayer of exorcism: the Litany of All Saints.

"Lord, have mercy."

"Christ have mercy."

"Lord, have mercy."

"Christ, hear us."

"God, the Father of heaven—"

Anna Ecklund, growing more agitated, suddenly growled. Or, rather, from somewhere inside her, the "growl" came. Never once, throughout the long exorcism, did her tongue or lips move. Now it was as if, to quote the observers, "a beast had wakened within her bowels." The sound "filled the room."

Father Theophilus raised his voice, "God, the Son, Redeemer of the world—"

Though surrounded by the taut, praying nuns the quivering woman suddenly "disengaged herself"—to quote the official record—"and with lightning speed, was carried through the air." She "landed" above the doorway of the old-fashioned, high-ceilinged room "and clung there with tenacious grip."

The Sisters shrieked—and stared at Anna Ecklund attached to the ceiling. For Father Theophilus, though, it was important that hysteria be stopped before it started.

"You must bring her down. And keep her down!"

They brought Anna Ecklund down—"with effort."

Once again on the bed, the woman gave a moan and sank into a heavy coma. She was to remain in that state for the rest of the exorcism, becoming unconscious each morning as the rite began, waking when the day's exhausting ordeal was done—remembering nothing.

Father Theophilus went back to his litany. At "God the Son, Redeemer of the world," "God the Holy Ghost," and "Holy Trinity, One God," the unconscious woman writhed and "a gnashing of teeth filled the room." With the three invocations to Mary, followed by "St. Michael the Archangel, pray for us," she subsided for the moment "as if struck by lightning."

Throughout the long and impressive litany—intoned in Latin, of course—her reactions varied as pleas went forth to the various heavenly powers. Mention of "Choirs" and "Holy Apostles" brought "muffled groaning." *"Ab insidiis diaboli"* ("From the snares of the devil") caused Anna Ecklund's body to jump convulsively. "Through Thy Cross and Passion" brought "moaning and yelping."

The exorcist's primary problem was to find out if one or more devils had taken possession of the woman. According to Church dogma, Satan can be made to speak, give answer, even to tell the truth—though, as the Father of Lies, he still remains expert at misleading and sidetracking. That is why the right choice of exorcist is so important.

Father Theophilus was a veteran. Before the first afternoon was over, he brought forth "voices." To state that everyone, except the experienced exorcist, was terrified, is putting it literally.

The nerve-wracking howls grew in volume. Despite the closed windows people came on the run, out of their homes and from nearby fields, till a sizeable crowd milled around the convent.

Farmers opined the screaming was of pigs being butchered in the old-fashioned, knife-sticking manner. Businessmen thought a nun had been murdered. A few instinctively guessed the truth. There was only one thing for the Church to do: admit that a case of exorcism was in progress and ask all people of good faith to pray for the tortured person.

In the initial stages the effects of the exorcism on Anna Ecklund were frightening. To begin with, the woman's body became grotesquely distorted, bloating until neither the Sisters nor Father Steiger could bear the sight. It was necessary for Father Theophilus to explain again and again that Satan would use every device within his power to make them call the whole thing off. He advised those present to take turns at getting outside into the fresh air—advice they accepted gratefully.

For his own protection (and with permission of the Bishop) the exorcist carried a consecrated Host in a pyx on his breast. The others had been certain the devil could not remain in the presence of what Catholics believe to be the actual Body and Blood of Christ, but the Capuchin set them straight.

"The devil approached Christ when He walked on earth, tempting and taunting Him. Now, as then, he is bold. But his outrages against the Host are limited."

Under Father Theophilus' insistence, the intermittent roaring in Anna Ecklund became, with dramatic suddenness, a recognizable voice. Asked "in the Name of Jesus, the Crucified Savior" if one or more spirits were involved in the case of possession, a voice from somewhere within the woman's body answered, "There are many!"

There followed another prolonged period of "ugly bellowing and howling" from the mute lips of the unconscious woman. Henceforth this occurred every day, "sometimes lasting for hours." A dozen nuns organized themselves into relays, so there was always a fresh group ready when Anna Ecklund needed them most.

And they were needed. For if the howling was unnerving, worse followed. The possessed woman began to froth, spit, vomit forth "unmentionable excrements"—as often as twenty times in a day. Though she was scarcely able to eat throughout the incredible ordeal (and then only light foods in the evenings after exorcism) unbelievable quantities of obnoxious matter poured from her. Some of it resembled "vomited macaroni," some "chewed and sliced tobacco leaves." Towards the end, the outpourings were such as were "humanly impossible to lodge in a human body."

Time and again Father Steiger and the horrified nuns were certain the woman was dying on their hands; and time and again Father Theophilus had to plead with them not to panic. This, he said, was the possessing devil's counter-attack. As for Anna Ecklund dying, he assured them the devil could not go that far.

From his viewpoint, he was making real progress by then. And, frightened though they were, the others recognized it also. They could clearly discern a number of "voices" amid the bellowing and moaning.

It was soon apparent that two basic types of demons possessed Anna Ecklund. Devils from the realm of fallen angels seemed "more reserved." In the presence of the Blessed Sacrament, they "howled mournfully, like whipped curs." Others—once the active souls of men on earth—were described as "bold and fearless." Once "raised," they caused the most violent excretions to come forth from the hapless woman "as if they would desecrate the Sacred Host but were unable to."

Now, under the pressure of exorcism, the first possessing demon suddenly gave voice. Herewith from the records: "In the Name of Jesus and His Most Blessed Mother, Mary the Incarnate, who crushes the serpent's head, tell me the truth!" thundered the old Capuchin. "Who is the leader or prince among you? What is your name?"

There came "a barking, as of a hound of hell." Then a "voice" said, "Beelzebub!"

"Lucifer, the prince of devils?"

"Not *the* prince. But one of the leaders."

"A fallen angel?"

There was "a snapping of teeth," then the admission: "That is right!"

"One of those whose pride made him want to be like God?"

The barking again, then a pronounced sneering. "We hate Him still."

"You must know that we will never stop now till the woman is free."

"I know more than you, that's certain!" Beelzebub's pride was stung. "I have not lost any knowledge or intellect, remember! You are hard to discourage, but this time you will not win."

It was too early for Father Theophilus to be worried. His next question was a superb stroke of spiritual swordsmanship—a thrust at the enemy's weak point, pride.

"Or do you hail from the lower angels?"

"You imbecile! I once belonged to the Seraphic Choir!"

"What would you do if God made it possible for you to atone for your injustice to Him?"

"You are a fool! Don't you know your theology?"

"All right. How long have you been torturing the unfortunate woman?"

"Since her fourteenth year."

"How dared you enter an innocent girl? How could you enter?"

There was a burst of derisive laughter, "Wouldn't you like to know!"

"I command you, in the Name of the Crucified Christ..."

"Lay off it! I've had enough of that for one day."

"Then tell me. Why?"

"Her own father cursed us into her!"

"And why did you, Beelzebub, choose to take possession?"

"You talk foolishly. Don't you get your orders?"

"Then you are here at the command of Lucifer?"

"How else?"

The Capuchin priest conversed with Beelzebub in English, German and Latin. The devil, like the others to follow, replied correctly in the tongue in which he was addressed. He was so language-perfect, in fact, that when Father Theophilus mispronounced an odd Latin word, Beelzebub shrieked corrections—and castigations. Asked why the father of Anna Ecklund had cursed her, Beelzebub muttered inarticulately. The tiring Capuchin turned to the parish priest.

"What did he say?"

The stunned Father Steiger had missed it, too. They turned to the nuns. "She gave him no peace, I think," one Sister volunteered.

"You lying little virgin!" Beelzebub howled, "Stick to the truth! I said: 'Leave me in peace.' Ask him yourself."

"I ask you this: is her father one of the devils within her now?"

There was a burst of "sneering laughter mixed with malicious joy."

"He is!"

"Since when?"

"Since the very moment of his damnation."

Demoniac laughter almost drowned out the strong voice of the exorcist. "I solemnly command, in the Name of the Crucified Savior of Nazareth, that you present the father of this woman and that he give me answer!"

A deep rough voice completely filled the room, terrorizing the nuns even more than the dialogue with Beelzebub.

"Are you," asked the exorcist, "the father who cursed his own child?"

There was a defiant roar, "No!"

The exorcist, it is recorded, was momentarily startled. "Then who are you? I command you to give answer, to speak the truth."

"I am Judas!"

"Judas Iscariot? The former apostle?"

The answer was an affirmative, howled in a bass voice so fearful that, this time, Father Steiger fled from the room—though most of the nuns stuck to their posts.

The exorcism lost ground and was resumed with another session of spitting and vomiting that, in turn, settled down to a long-drawn battle of endurance. Like Beelzebub before him, however, Judas too was forced to give answer.

The recorded dialogue revealed that the chief mission of Judas was to bring Anna Ecklund to despair. "To cause her to commit suicide. To make her hang herself."

"But you cannot?"

"We might have if you hadn't interfered."

"Might have?"

"She has free will." There was a stream of "shocking" curses; Judas' frustration was evident. When Father Theophilus interrupted him, he raved anew over his mission. "She must get a rope. She must savor it around her neck!"

"Is it true that everyone who commits suicide goes to hell?"

"That would be nice. But it's not."

"Why not?"

The gist of Judas' answer was that, in many cases, the devils overdo their tempting, destroying the element of the victim's deliberate choice. The memory of being thus cheated caused another infernal moaning.

Father Theophilus questioned Judas about the betrayal of Christ.

Judas cursed horribly. "Don't talk about that!"

"Don't you regret committing the despicable deed?"

Another "terrible curse"—not given in the records—followed. "I said don't talk about that. I made my choice. Leave me alone."

At about this stage, Lucifer himself became manifest—though, from the accounts, he seemed to inject himself at will, sometimes silencing his subordinates, sometimes throwing the whole ritual into reverse gear. At such times, "countless brats of devils" interrupted the exorcism "by their disagreeable and almost unendurable interferences."

Lucifer's presence was always dramatically marked—not by a smell of fire and brimstone but by swarms of "avenging spirits" filled with hatred and anger against all human beings. Satan boasted they were "powers of discord"—able to magnify small grievances into mountains, to set a parish against its pastor, brother against brother, man against wife.

Lucifer, throughout, showed himself a master of retort and a wily tactician. His objective obviously was to frighten the participants, to delay the inquisition, to exhaust the exorcist and thus to prevent him from driving out his (Lucifer's) established forces.

During his presence, Anna Ecklund's face became so distorted that her features were unrecognizable. The "vilest of stenches—the odor of hell" filled the room so that even the nursing nuns gagged and fled outside for air.

Mrs. Ecklund's body, at first thin and emaciated, now bloated up hideously, till the terrified Sisters thought it would burst.

The only answer Father Theophilus made to these attacks was prolonged personal prayer mixed with persistent exorcism. Approaching with a Relic of the Cross and intoning the prescribed words: "Look on the wood of the Cross! Begone, Satan! Begone, all ye powers of hell!" he again and again forced Lucifer into temporary retreat, leaving the exorcist free to do battle with the established devils.

Apparently various parts of the rite affected Lucifer differently than the possessing demons. The pronouncement, "A *spiritu fornicationis, libera nos, Dominel*" ("From the spirit of uncleanliness, Lord, deliver us!") produced desperate "squirming" of the possessed woman's body.

"Through Thy Cross and Passion," brought forth the by-now-familiar moaning and yelping. The injunction, "I command you in the name of the Immaculate Conception, in the name of Her who crushes the serpent's head," produced a sudden "languishing" of his activities. "He relaxed," says the account, "as one mortally stunned." To a layman, his status as resident is confusing. Apparently he was not a "possessing" spirit but a visiting general. The impression is that abiding demons are localized in their activities, while Lucifer needs freedom of movement—to be "abroad."

"How else," he asked once, "am I to organize the Anti-Christ?"

When Father Theophilus asked why he persisted in such a "useless" battle (presumably the battle of the ages—not the localized struggle over Anna Ecklund) Lucifer was unusually sardonic.

"Useless? It's a matter of viewpoint." The whole issue, Satan added, had begun "before the ages began," in accordance with "set laws."

Unlike the special demons, Lucifer refused to talk much about his own particular past. He refused also to listen to the prayer beginning, "St. Michael the Archangel, defend us in the day of battle! Be our protection against the wickedness and snares of the devil." Presumably its historic overtones rankled.

Lucifer's reaction to various sacramental acts varied considerably. The sprinkling of Anna Ecklund's body with holy water, for instance, brought blood-curdling screams. A cross, made of papier-mâché (as the surprised exorcist discovered later) brought derisive laughter. "If I remember correctly, 'He' died, rather ignobly, on a wooden cross."

Father Theophilus asked, "You were there?"

For his curiosity, he got two hours of blood-curdling laughter.

Lucifer adopted an injured air over the attitude of modern religionists. He challenged anyone to deny he had ever disappointed anyone open-minded enough to concede his power. Some he had showered with the kingdoms of the world.

"But," queried Father Theophilus, "what of eternity?"

"Nan ad rem!" ("Not to the point!") Satan snapped.

If he was curt with the exorcist, he unleashed torrents of contempt on Father Steiger. Never a day passed without his berating the pastor for permitting the exorcism at all—and his threats were very real to any priest. Finally he laid down his ultimatum. Either Father Steiger called the whole thing off, or "I'll incite the whole parish against you," presumably through the "avenging demons."

Actually, Father Steiger was then laboring under tremendous doubts. He was worried. What were people saying and thinking, especially after these days of horrible screaming from the convent? The more the pastor brooded, the more his distaste for the whole affair grew. It seemed, somehow, grossly indecent.

He even began to doubt his own sanity. The thought struck him, finally, that anyone able to produce this sort of supernatural horror might even be a devil himself.

At the end of another day's exorcism he waited outside the rectory for the Capuchin's return, wondering if he should order Father Theophilus out of the parish entirely before the whole affair became a national scandal.

"After you've had your supper," Father Steiger began coldly, "I think we had better do some serious talking."

For Father Theophilus eating was, by now, almost impossible. He turned his tired blue eyes on the man who had been his lifelong friend. "Don't you see, Father? That is all he needs now, to win."

It was a critical moment in the case, but after praying at some length, Father Steiger thought he did discern the strategy.

The next time he entered the convent room, Lucifer broke off his current subject to berate him worse than before. "So you wouldn't have it the easy way? Then suffer!"

For Father Steiger, it was exactly what he needed. He stiffened. "You can't harm me," he said in defiance of Lucifer. "I stand now under the protection of Christ Himself—"

"I can't?" The devil was beside himself, "I've had better priests than you shot down on their own altars. And I hung Him on a Cross!"

The exorcist tried to intervene. "Leave the pastor alone! I am the one who fights you—not he!"

"He gave permission!" There was a burst of the sharper laughter, indicative of Lucifer's particular annoyance. "And he shall pay for it—on Friday!"

The following Friday as he was finishing breakfast there was an urgent sick call for Father Steiger. The mother of a farmer-parishioner was seriously ill. The farmer's car refused to start. Could Father Steiger take his own car?

And could he please hurry?

Father Steiger's car was new—a surprise gift from his flock—and he knew every foot of the road. But for the first time in his life he did not hurry to administer Extreme Unction.

Returning later along the same dirt road he drove even more slowly. Approaching a bridge near Earling he was suddenly aware of a "black cloud" blotting out first the guard-rails, then the entire outline of the bridge. He threw the car into low gear. Even so, it "hurled itself" towards the cloud.

A farmer, hearing the crash, hurriedly left his work. He found the car a shambles, the steering wheel smashed.

Then he saw Father Steiger crawling out of the wreckage. The farmer drove the priest to Earling where the doctor found "some external scars and a state of nervous excitement." Otherwise, Father Steiger was unhurt.

A stubborn Teuton at heart, the priest headed straight for the convent. The instant he entered Anna Ecklund's room uproarious laughter upset the exorcism again.

"Rather proud of that new car, weren't you, boy? How do you like it now?"

As it turned out, the sympathetic (and prosperous) farmers of Earling were to buy Father Steiger a new car; but the devil kept raising the incident and promising "more fun."

It came—in rat-like noises in the night, slamming doors and sudden "movements" of his bed that brought him awake with the sweat standing on his skin. He finally resorted to reciting the "small office" of exorcism, which eventually stopped those disturbances.

Other priests—a number were permitted to watch the exorcism—reported similar noises and experiences. They, too, took to sleeping with holy water and stola nearby.

Then Lucifer suddenly opened a new attack. He threatened to disclose "rather embarrassing" details from out of the past lives of those taking active part in the exorcism. When Father Theophilus warned them to stand their ground, he proceeded to make good his threat.

"You remember, Sister," he addressed one of the more reserved nuns by name, "the summer you were eleven years old?"

The Sister was startled—and suddenly scarlet-faced.

"No need to be *that* embarrassed," said the devil smoothly. "Just leave and we can drop the whole incident."

Nuns don't get to be nuns, however, without learning courage and discipline. "I had forgotten that!" whispered the stricken Sister. Then, with feminine defiance: "If you're going to bring up the sins of my childhood, go ahead! Why don't you tell everyone those of my adult years?"

"Unfortunately," said Lucifer calmly, "what you have confessed, I have no way of knowing."

To the Catholic chroniclers this was an "astonishing admission" though it undoubtedly explains, at least in part, why the rubrics in the Roman ritual for exorcism demand a general confession beforehand on the part of all those involved in a case.

The record makes clear that Satan did know, with the exception of "sins confessed," all the human vanities and weaknesses of those present. His strategy was to scandalize, shock and immobilize the group—and apparently it came close to succeeding.

Certain now that Satan was outdoing himself for a purpose more important than the shielding of Beelzebub, Judas and scores of lesser spirits, the old Capuchin concentrated everything on Lucifer in person.

The enemy yelled, howled, worked hideous physical phenomena—but stuck stubbornly to his position for almost two solid weeks—by which time the indomitable Capuchin's suspicions were verified. Even the others were aware now that, in the person of Anna Ecklund, two more powerful devils were entrenched. On them, the Capuchin was at last able to concentrate his fire.

They came forth amid clouds of "dumb devils," more pestering than powerful, who caused a confusion of sounds but were easily driven away by the commands of the exorcist, only to return again and again—frustrating and wearying the exorcist.

By this time, in fact, Father Theophilus was on the verge of a physical breakdown. The case had become so drawn-out and critical that, in a move unprecedented in modern times, the pastor received permission to ask publicly for prayers, fasting and penance on the part of the local parishioners. Everyone in the vicinity of Earling now knew that an exorcism was going on in their midst. Even the busy farmers flocked to morning Mass and evening devotions—and Father Theophilus continued his task with what strength he had left.

The next demon yielded, like the others, under the familiar prayers of exorcism. As in the case of Judas, the listeners could tell by his voice that he had once been a human being. The exorcist ordered him to reveal his name.

"Jacob."

"Which Jacob?"

"Her father!"

The Rev. Theophilus Riesinger was anything but bashful in his probing. The record of the exorcism simply condenses a hair-raising story of a life completely irreligious, coarse, brutal, and "loathsomely unchaste," culminating in Jacob's repeated attempts to force his daughter, Anna, to commit incest with him.

"And she would not?"

Anna would not. In fact, on the last occasion of her refusal, she threatened to tell her mother, the priest and everyone else what he wanted of her. The enraged Jacob cursed her—"I willed the devils in hell to enter into her and drive her to abominations."

"How old was she then?"

"Fourteen."

"You—her own father—"

The exorcist was stopped with an unprecedented torrent of filth, spittle and excrement. That day he changed apparel four times, drove back the swarms of dumb devils, and kept forcing Jacob to answer.

In a long drawn-out explanation Jacob conveyed the information that he might have been saved in spite of all, that he might, at the last moment, have received enough grace for repentance, except for the unforgivable crime of "giving" his child to the devils. That determined his damnation.

"And even yet you want to torture her, knowing that your own punishment is forever?"

"Till her end!" The intensity of Jacob's hate made the nuns tremble—literally.

"Satan commanded you to dwell in your own child?"

"I wished that, too. Satan rejoiced when I burned to enter into her."

The exorcist's voice stiffened, "The power of Christ Crucified and of the Blessed Trinity will force you from her forever—force you back into the pit where you belong!"

"No! No!" Jacob's "voice" rose like that of an animal in death-agony. "Spare me that! You who call yourself a man of mercy—No!"

The Capuchin's sympathies lay with the unconscious woman who had begged so long for someone to help her; who now lay helpless, dependent on him.

There was still another demon to come, one whose falsetto voice had been discernible alongside Jacob's. On her, Father Theophilus now concentrated the ritual of exorcism.

The most hateful of all in her replies—causing hideous vomiting from

Anna Ecklund—she finally spat forth the admission that her name was Mina.

"Mina" meant nothing to anyone there. Father Theophilus pressed the question.

"Mina, the mistress of Jacob."

"You are damned because of your affair with him?"

Forced to talk, she revealed that, round for round, her life had been as repulsive as Jacob's. It had been a classic of sodomy.

"This was the specific cause of your damnation?"

Mina admitted worse—"unrepented" child murder.

"Who did you kill?"

Bitterness filled Mina's voice, "Little ones."

"How many?"

"Three. No! Four."

"You were a Catholic?"

From Beelzebub to Mina, Father Theophilus had to find out why they had lost their souls. "Couldn't you have gone to Confession, made your peace with God?"

Mina went on to reveal flashes of a life as horribly sacrilegious as Jacob's. Unworthy Communions turned out to be the deciding cause of her damnation, then of her torment. The Host—as with Jacob—was the object of her burning hatred. The filth she brought forth from the body of Anna Ecklund was designed to desecrate.

These two demons, once human, were the most diabolically dedicated in their hatreds and obscenities.

For Father Theophilus there remained the last exhausting act of the exorcism—to drive these permanent, possessing devils from Anna Ecklund forever. Although obviously weakened, the demons begged not to be dispossessed, and their "groans and anguish" apparently had heart-rending effects on the witnesses.

By now the exorcist was working in a state of almost complete exhaustion (so much so, says the account, that he feared for his own life). He had been laboring without letup for twenty days, a period unprecedented in the history of the Catholic Church. In appearance he had aged twenty years.

Though Father Steiger could no longer do without a solid night's sleep, though the alternating shifts of Sisters were so tired as to be moving in a semi-stupor, he, Father Theophilus, now stepped up his efforts. So far, the exorcism had gone on from dawn till dusk each day. Now it would go day and night, around the clock, till either he dropped or the demons departed.

Again the Catholics of Earling and nearby parishes were urged to help by constant prayer, fasting and vigils. Again they flocked to the churches. The interest of the Church in the case was so widespread that even a Bishop in Switzerland was following it anxiously.

The stepped-up exorcism had noticeable effect. Lucifer was less active personally; any of the four major devils could be called and mauled at will. Instead of the roaring and defiance, their voices were "pitiful and pleading" now.

"Spare us! Stop torturing us!"

"Depart!"

"We will be driven back to hell."

"But you're in hell now!"

Apparently they weren't—at least not literally. By their explanation, they were "of hell"; hell "is constantly with us"; but it was "tremendous relief" to be able to roam the earth, working hatred and malice, plotting and inciting the captivity of souls.

They were willing to talk, talk, talk—but not to depart.

For seventy-two hours without letup, they pleaded that it would be "more bearable" to be in another person, another place, anywhere rather than to be driven back down to the region of infernal torment, to give an account of their ultimate failure.

If Father Theophilus was teetering on the brink of collapse, the demons were likewise weakening rapidly. The end was near. Father Theophilus, advancing with the Cross, heard their cry of capitulation at last.

"No! Enough! We will go back!"

Father Theophilus, hard put to whisper, suspected a last and final deceit: a pretense on the part of the Big Four to leave the possessed, then a stealthy return when the exorcism ended.

"In the Name of the Most Blessed Trinity, I command that you give me a sign of your leave-taking forever."

There was a last murmur of uneasiness, then a demand from Beelzebub as to the "sign."

"As you leave, you will each one call his name, departing never to return."

It was almost nine o'clock in the evening.

Suddenly on the bed, the body of Anna Ecklund, inert for hours, "broke from the grip of her protectors." She stood upright, only her heels touching the covers, and for a horrifying moment those present thought she would spring for the ceiling again.

But Father Theophilus knew victory when he saw it. From his worn Capuchin habit, the old priest drew forth his missionary's cross.

"Depart, ye fiends of hell! I conjure you, in the Name of Almighty God, in the Name of the Crucified Jesus of Nazareth, in the name of His purest mother, in the name of the Archangel Michael—begone, all ye powers of Satan! The Lion of Judah reigns!"

Anna Ecklund fell back on the bed. A piercing sound filled the room, causing all to tremble violently. In and over the sound came the "moan of many voices":

"Beelzebub! Judas! Jacob! Mina!" Then, as from a far distance, the voices wailed together: "Hell! Hell ... hell. Beelzebub ... Judas ... Jacob ... Mina ..."

Suddenly in the Convent of the Franciscan Sisters at Earling there was no sound except the heavy breathing of the old Capuchin. He turned to the bed.

Anna Ecklund was resting "like a child of twelve." She opened her eyes, tried to smile. "God bless you," Anna Ecklund said wearily.

The nuns began to weep. For a moment they were "scarcely aware" of the vile odor that again filled the room—"an unearthly, unbearable stench."

"Their parting gift," said Father Theophilus. "Open the windows. Air the convent. It is ended."

In Earling, Iowa, it was exactly 9:00 p.m., September 23rd, 1928—twenty-three days after the Rite of Exorcism began.

Anna Ecklund went home in peace, to "an untroubled life." No one, save the exorcist and a handful of those concerned, ever knew her real name—and the few who did kept it under a silence as binding as that of the confessional.

Someday, when man is done exploring basic laws of physics, he may get down to laws more primary still; laws studied so far only by theologians and mystics. If and when he does, the case of Anna Ecklund will be a classic.

This incredible drama would most certainly never have become known had it not been for its unforeseen violence and duration.

The Church presumably made its own analysis and prepared to bury it. But the affair continued to create such a sensation that almost seven years later, on July 23, 1935, the Most Reverend Jos. F. Busch, Bishop of St. Cloud, Minn., placed the *Imprimatur* on an approved summary of the case. This was an English translation, by the Rev. Celestine Kapsner, O.S.B., of St. John's Abbey, Collegeville, Minn., of an earlier account set down in German by the Rev. Carl Vogl. Everyone concerned was fully aware that the move was completely unprecedented. The Earling case remains the only exorcism case on which even a semi-detailed account has ever been made public by the Church of Rome.

Among the many who publicly testified to the authenticity of Father Kapsner's document was a highly-respected Milwaukee physician and surgeon, Dr. John Dundon, who declared Father Theophilus "a pious priest very gifted in a specialty which should command the patronage of the medical profession, rather than be allotted to the realm of superstition or necromancy."

By this time, of course, the Rev. Theophilus Riesinger had long since tucked his great crucifix back into his Capuchin robes and taken his leave of Earling. By 1935 he had performed nineteen exorcisms, a record unparalleled in modern times.

♪

IS YOUR DOG SMARTER THAN YOU ARE?

Marjorie MacCreary

I live with a genius! I do not refer to a friend, husband, or other relative, but to a four-year-old black dog whose name is Penny.

Newsmen have nicknamed him variously "mathematical mutt," "a midget in a fur coat," and "a length of stove pipe with legs."

A mixture of cocker and beagle, he was born on the farm of John Boos, near Huron, Ohio. Miss Caroline Monks, of Cleveland, owns him.

This four-footed mind-reader can do any mathematical problem his mistress can do, and since she is a mathematics teacher in Cleveland, this is no mean feat. He can subtract, multiply, divide, do square roots and, of course, add—provided the answer is a number no higher than twelve. Penny feels not even a piece of cheese is worth any additional effort.

Can you do this college algebra problem in one minute? Penny can and does—this and many others even more difficult.

"A's daily wage is twelve dollars less than B receives for four days. A receives ten dollars more for five days than B does in six days. Find the daily wage of each."

When the problem is read to him the little black dog sits up straight, his back as stiff as a ramrod, as he eyes the piece of cheese a few inches above his head. He could easily take it but he has learned to earn it.

His teacher asks, "What is the daily wage of A?"

Penny barks eight times and reaches for the cheese. There is no signal, for the dog knows when he has given the right answer.

His teacher continues, "What is the daily wage of B?"

"Arf, arf, arf, arf, arf."

Again the dog barks, pauses, and reaches for the cheese.

Penny will do equally well when the answer is written on a piece of paper. Unerringly, he barks the correct number of times.

No one is more surprised at this feat than we are. Only last February, we discovered that his trick of barking the right number of times was not the recognition of words, as we thought, but extrasensory perception of the number that was in our minds.

Wil Hane of the *Lorain Journal* said, "I saw it and I still don't believe it."

THE WORLD'S STRANGEST TRUE ENCOUNTERS

The dog's publicity started when we had Penny at the home of Elthelberta Hartman, who writes a column for several local papers. We fed Penny cheese, while Mrs. Hartman's grandchildren watched and even gave numbers to the dog. We were astonished when she wrote up the feat for her column.

Newsmen and photographers from the *Lorain Journal* and the *Cleveland News* invaded my summer cottage at Huronia Beach. They came with the expectation of proving Penny's performance was a trick. Mr. Eddie Dark of the *News* wanted to pose the dog beside the telephone and use the caption, "It's a phoney." But after he had written a number on paper, he found that there was no trick. Mr. E. Allen Knight said in his article, "By this time, it wouldn't have been hard for me and Eddie to believe we heard a *sotto voce* 'gimme the cheese.'"

Caroline Monks and I are equally surprised at the ability of the dog. He is definitely a dumb animal, in that be does not have the power of speech, but he has a sixth sense for understanding the thoughts of humans. This understanding is not limited to the English language. Our discovery of his unusual mental telepathy came when we found the butcher was giving him multiplication problems in Russian.

"He can't do that!" his mistress exclaimed.

"He's been doing it for a year," Mr. Kata replied, "not only in Russian but also in several other languages."

I should have guessed it! Several times a week I walk down to Kata's market to get groceries and meat for our dinner. I usually take the dog for they are always glad to see him. The butcher takes the leash, puts the dog through his tricks for the customers, and rewards the dog with pieces of cold cuts. The customers of our little suburb get into the act, while I make my purchases. Since his mistress teaches all day, I take care of the dog, as well as of two cats, and get dinner for all of us.

Penny takes a very maternal attitude toward the two cats. The three wait in a line, like a cafeteria, while my calico female eats. She is followed by Petey, the black and white kitten. After the dog has eaten he polishes the dish, washes the floor, and even licks Petey's white shirt front.

Penny also has a strong sense of ownership. He has his own ball, which he chases and fetches, and the cats have their roll of tinfoil. He never touches their toys and growls if they even approach his playthings.

Children are welcome, unless they touch his belongings. After one mistake, Penny barks every time he sees the offending child on the street.

I shall never forget my first sight of Penny. We had driven over to the farm to see the new litter of puppies and the twenty-two cats and kittens. Caroline had always wanted a dog but she had to wait fifty years for her first pet.

Waddling out of the barn came a handful of shiny black fur with feet so enormous the puppy kept tripping over them. No one could resist those big brown eyes and funny floppy ears! I preferred cats, so I took a calico kitten.

For six weeks, until the middle of June, we were weekend mothers. When we drove into the yard on Friday nights tiny, awkward Penny would run out of the barn barking excitedly. At the cottage, the puppy and kitten slept in one box beside the fire. Both ate from one dish, the cat liking dog food and the dog drinking milk.

Penny's fondness for milk greatly embarrassed us one day. We drove into the farmyard just at the cats' mealtime. All twenty-two kittens were waiting for the big pan of milk which supplemented their diet of field mice. As the huge pan was placed on the ground, Penny jumped out of the car and drank all the milk under the noses of the cats.

Penny's beagle blood makes him a good watch dog. He will defend us and the cats against any danger. Once Petey got out of my cottage and we couldn't find him anywhere. Penny, with his hound nose to the ground, led us to a little clearing. Here little Petey was bristling for battle against a huge yellow tom, whose nightly fights disturbed the neighborhood. Penny growled and took his place beside our cat. The yellow tom remembered a previous appointment—hurriedly.

Actually, we never have been able to convince Penny that he is a dog. I lift his silky, black ear and whisper, "You're a dog!" He looks at me indignantly and walks away. Dogs, he feels, are terrible creatures who go around biting humans. In the car, he warns us at sight of a D-O-G. We once spelled words to conceal our thoughts. Now we talk to him as though he understood us. From his response, I'm sure he does.

Penny's profession, if you call it that, is Watch Dog for us and the cats. While I write in my study, Penny watches for the "cookie" man, whom he welcomes. The mailman is on his blacklist, since he is often followed by a collie. The garbage men throw him into a frenzy, since they remove the metal can into which go chicken bones, meat fat, and other things not on a dog's diet.

Unfortunately, Penny is an exhibitionist. Dearly loving to show his ability in mathematics, he quivers with anticipation, his eyes fixed on his teacher and his nostrils quivering at the smell of the cheese. If the problem is slow in being given, he begins to bark, so as not to waste time in getting the cheese. As for his musical ability, he will sing *Home, Sweet Home!* only behind closed doors.

Penny's intelligence has no relation to his formal education. Like many dogs, he attended an obedience class of the Western Reserve Kennel Club, placing third in a class of twenty. His mathematical ability developed two years later.

His ability to give the correct number of barks to a problem is in no way unusual, since most dogs read their masters' minds. While their masters think that dogs understand words, they actually read thoughts.

Experiments in extrasensory perception are being carried on at Duke University and at other institutions both here and abroad. In his article in the *American Weekly* of February 16, 1958, Dr. J. B. Rhine discusses this human power, especially as it is manifested in the relationship between teacher and pupil. One Dutch school supervisor in Amsterdam started this study with a series of tests designed to determine whether teachers actually give their pupils answers in class.

I am a former teacher and I believe this may have some basis. While pupils do well in class work, especially in mathematics, languages, or formal grammar, later in doing their homework they complain that they "understood it in class." Their minds had followed the steps in reasoning with the mind of the teacher and not independently. Living, as he does, with two teachers, Penny has become responsive to this mind-reading.

I do not pretend to be scientific about this subject on the basis of one dog's ability to bark correct answers. Conclusive results can come only from objective, controlled tests. However, several aspects of the dog's behavior convince me that his so-called mathematical ability is pure mind-reading. For four years, I have observed his habits.

First, animals are thought to have no number sense, except possibly some birds that seem to know when there is an egg missing from the nest. Surely counting requires a much higher level of intelligence than we can expect in a dog.

Second, whatever language is used seems immaterial. Penny has done problems in Russian, French, German and other languages, just as quickly and correctly as in English.

Third, the mental concentration and attitude of the person who is giving the problem is important. After seeing the dog perform several times the reporter from the *News* tried it himself. When the dog was confused we realized that the reporter thought that it was a trick and that no stranger could do it. When we finally convinced him, he concentrated on the thoughts he was giving to the dog, both by word and by writing the number on paper, with the result that he got a perfect performance every time.

Fourth, for this reason, younger children are not always successful with Penny. They are not always capable of this concentration and their slowness in giving the problems makes the dog too eager. If the dog does not get the problem rapidly enough, he begins barking too soon.

Moreover, he will pause between the two numbers in addition. Thus, if a teacher gives him five and two, he barks five times, pauses, and then barks twice. For a long time, this made us think there was an association of words.

Fifth, Penny's comprehension of our thoughts is not limited to numbers. If we reprove the cats for anything the dog also punishes them. Like most dogs, he is suspicious of callers, until they are welcomed. In his short life, he has lived in seven different houses and yet can go to any room we mention. Moreover, from a row of ten toys, he will unerringly choose the one we name.

Most of these characteristics are true of thousands of dogs, who understand their masters better than their masters understand them. However, dogs, like children, possess wills of their own to resist a command they consider irrational or to assert their personalities. Thus, a dog will go to his dish when he is told but unless he is hungry he will not eat.

Penny is not remarkable in most ways—he is just better understood. While neither Miss Monks nor I want Penny to become a theatrical performer, we are glad that his publicity has brought a better understanding of dogs. Perhaps it will also bring about a better understanding of the unlimited possibilities for practical use of extrasensory perception.

We may even learn to be as smart as our dogs and to read their minds.

"HELP ME TO BE FREE!"

Alicia Brade

When Sobrina left me at seven o'clock on that bright spring morning in the tiny village in South America I could not know that I would not see her again "in the flesh." The next time I talked with Sobrina it was with her spiritual self; her earthly body lay in a casket, piled high with flowers, on the very spot where I had parted with her so short a time before.

Sobrina and I had had great plans. We were going to travel; we were going to see the whole world. But these dreams were never to be realized, for Sobrina was killed, the victim of a cruel accident, a seemingly senseless accident. She stepped into the path of an escaped prisoner who was fleeing from the police. With no intent to harm her, he pushed her to one side. Unfortunately he had in his hand a very sharp knife, and Sobrina died.

That is what her friends and her family thought. But I know otherwise, for I talked with her and I was able to help her after her death. This story is not concerned with the manner of Sobrina's death so much as with what happened afterward.

I first knew Sobrina when she attended my class to learn to speak English. She was a teacher and wished to study our schools so she might go home and improve her own country. She was a dedicated person. I helped her meet people who could help her, and when the time came for her to return to her country she invited me to go with her. It seemed such a worthy cause, and at the time I was free to leave, so I accompanied her and we became co-workers in an unofficial manner. We worked together for nearly five years, she as planner and organizer, I as advisor and "moral support."

Despite our close business association we never became in any sense closely bound either mentally or spiritually, I thought. I learned it was truly otherwise, but only after she was "dead."

Outwardly, Sobrina would give no hint of softness. She did not go to church and I doubt that she thought herself capable of believing in a supreme being. Nor would she admit of any sentimental feeling toward any living creature, human or animal. However, her friends saw below the surface, for they sincerely adored her.

You will realize, then, something of the shock I experienced as I watched the preparations for her funeral after returning from the hospital where I had arrived too late to help Sobrina. The bedroom and living room, or *sala,* had been stripped of everything. They were completely bare. In the center of the *sala* the casket was supported on a high base. Black ruffled streamers were strung from the central overhead light to the four ceiling corners, creating a wide canopy. At the head of the casket stood a tall crucifix, and around the casket were placed seven-foot high candles. Great wreaths began to arrive, and with them came mounds of lilies to be piled high on top of the casket. People swarmed everywhere, silently weeping or crying hysterically.

I watched in silence, knowing how Sobrina would have felt about all this ritual. I took comfort in the thought that Sobrina could not know of it. How wrong I was!

All through the night of mourning I moved from person to person, patting a shoulder here and murmuring comfort there. Mounds of cakes and sandwiches, gallons of coffee were served throughout the night. At dawn the friends departed to assume the duties of the day. At nightfall of the second day they would return to sit again in the silent corridors and patio.

Within the room where Sobrina lay throughout the night, groups of black clad women had knelt in prayer. Endless rosaries had been said in a continuous murmur.

Because there was little that I could do, I had slipped away for a few moments of quiet within my own room. It was then that she called me—as she had done every evening when she came home from work. I heard her clearly. *"La comida esta servida.* Come on, Meesus Bee."

I went to the dining area and spoke with the only person who understood English. "Did you call me?" I asked. "No," she replied, "but you should eat, for there will be much to face before the night is over."

So Sobrina had got in touch with me after all; my heart leaped with joy. I sat down and ate. Sobrina was not in her chair but she was there!

The next morning I sat in the corridor thinking about this. Across from me, through the open door, Sobrina lay. I marveled at the number of wreaths, flowers and telegrams that had arrived during the night. It was then that Sobrina called me again.

"Meesus Bee. Come here and *help* me!" How often I had heard such a call, in just such a voice. It seemed to come from her own room, where her bed had been before the rooms were cleared. I went, however, and stood by the casket. For the first time I saw her, and so natural she looked, so asleep, so like I had seen her a thousand times, that I was startled. However, as I watched the tranquil slumbering face I saw another Sobrina superimposed above her earthly form. Even while her earthly body lay immobile, expressionless, another Sobrina, a spiritual body, struggled and twisted.

"What is it, Sobrina?" I asked.

"I don't know what the trouble is," she replied in great distress. "I can't get my eyes open."

Sobrina apparently thought she was in her bed. Conscious of the fact that it was time to get up she was making a mighty effort to do so. I hastened to reassure her. "You don't need to get up, Sobrina. Lie back and rest. Just keep your eyes closed. Lie still; don't try to open your eyes."

Her earth body remained quiet in the casket, but the ethereal Sobrina, which I could see superimposed above the body, was now asleep in her own bed.

Sabrina did not know that she was dead!

I returned to the corridor. Groups of people were arriving, first rosaries were being murmured. I had had many previous contacts with persons who had "died." I had talked with persons who were still troubled by earthly affairs left unfinished, and had been able to help free them from their worries. I had talked with many who didn't know that they were "dead," who were bewildered and hurt because they could not make contact with the people around them. These I had been able to help, not by telling them that they were "dead" but by explaining their changed state, that they would not be able to do the things they had formerly done, nor in the same manner. But I had never been present when somebody tried to get up and walk! I had read of such things—amazing instances of dead persons lifting an arm, opening the eyes, turning in the casket. Usually such incidents are called "muscular contraction." Now I knew better.

Sobrina called me again. I hastened to her side. Momentarily the space around the casket was free of people. I spoke to her again.

"What is it now?" I asked in dismay, for I could see that she was making a fierce struggle to free herself from some bond that seemed to hold her. "What is the trouble?" I asked.

She was indignant this time. "I can't get my eyes open!" she stormed. "What is the matter? I must get up!"

"Sobrina, Sobrina!" I spoke sharply and aloud, for there was no one near. "Sobrina! Listen! You must not try to get up! Believe me, you must not!"

But Sobrina continued to struggle against the unseen bonds that held her. "Let me up, let me up," she insisted.

I resorted to pleading "Sobrina," I said, "you have been hurt. You must rest. You don't need your eyes, now. You will have better ones. Everything you have ever wanted you will have, believe me. You have wanted to travel; now you will. You will go everywhere." She quieted. Her angry voice changed to a low complaint.

"Who are all these people?" she demanded. "What are they doing here? Please send them away. They bother me! Please make them go! They are making too much noise!"

The room was filled once more with people; a kneeling circle of women were again saying their rosaries. I stood my ground at the side of her casket and continued to talk mentally with her. "They don't mean any harm," I said. I was filled with a sudden fear that she might realize what was taking place. If Sobrina ever became aware that all this ritualistic commotion was over her, she would, I was almost certain, arise and scatter the people in terror. "Sobrina," I pleaded. "Please take my word for it. Everything is all right. Don't struggle. Just let go. Just—go to sleep."

It was then that I realized to what extent she relied upon me. She accepted with a sigh and lay back. Quickly, as if an invisible anesthetic cone had been slipped over her face, she sank back inert. Sobrina would struggle no more, I felt certain. I left the room, shaken but grateful.

About eleven o'clock I was called again, but not by Sobrina. I stepped to the side of the casket to observe spirit workers caring for Sobrina. They were trying to loosen her soul from the hard shell that encased it. Above the casket I could see all this, above the slumbering body of Sobrina. It was a shell such as the cocoon of a moth. Along the top it had been cracked and inside I could see the beautiful white silk that encased her real soul. Within I could see Sobrina twisting and turning, making determined attempts to free herself from the binding shell. She was fully conscious of what she was doing and she was eager to show me that she was trying. "I'm working on it," she said grimly. I gave her a nod of approval.

I watched the entire process. I saw the white silk wrappings raised high above the cocoon, where it swung in a hammock of fine threads. Guiding hands were shaking it gently as though to break it loose without injury. The cocoon that had enclosed it now shriveled, for it was being consumed by white hot, tiny flames that burned below it. I realized that all that was mortal would soon be reduced to ashes, and I realized at that moment what a blessing cremation of the body can be if the escaping soul can be protected from the shock of realization. Once burned in this white fire the body is beyond harm and there is nothing left to be concerned over.

When a person who has "died is shocked suddenly into the realization of death great consternation, even terror may come. This makes it difficult for "the angels in charge" to render proper assistance. A soul may become so fearful that it refuses to go on and endless delay results. In many instances, perhaps in most, the person who has "died" is not aware of it, and to become aware naturally arouses the desire to remain with the loved ones who so reluctantly release their hold. In this manner souls are "earth bound." Don't do this to the ones you love.

Funeral ceremonies should be held in quietness, with the assurance that your loved one is not gone, but changed. We do not die. We pass into another phase of existence.

If this story makes easier the passing of a few souls, it has been worth the telling. Sobrina had a mission; perhaps this message is a part of it.

When last I saw the silk-wrapped soul of Sobrina it was white and shining, high above the casket, still in its hammock of silken threads. As I watched, it righted itself and began to spin swiftly and, thus spinning, it rose higher and higher. Sobrina had no further need for struggle. She was carried gently and swiftly out of my sight. My eyes dropped back to the casket; the space above it was now empty. All signs of Sobrina were gone—except for the silent form in the casket that now had assumed the appearance of death.

"Goodbye," I whispered. *"Vaya con Dios."*

THE MISSING CREW OF THE AIRSHIP L-8

William O. Foss

The U.S. Navy, which has had its share of strange mystery ships, has added another such story to the historical sea chest—only this story isn't about a crewless ship but about a crewless airship, the L-8.

Airship L-8 joined the mysteries when it flew out over the California coastline on a routine submarine patrol during World War II. Five hours after takeoff she bounced back to earth—without a sign of her two-man crew.

The unsolved riddle of Airship L-8 began twenty-five years ago, at 6:00 a.m. of August 16, 1942, at Treasure Island Naval Base in San Francisco.

Two young naval aviators, Lieutenant (junior grade) Ernest D. Cody and Ensign Charles E. Adams of Airship Squadron 32, listened to last minute instructions from their flight operations officer.

The weather was cloudy and the traditional California morning dew blanketed the coast. Such a static condition made the airship a bit heavy on weigh-off, and for that reason only Cody and Adams would make the flight. Normally a third man went along on such patrol flights, but the heavy, damp air grounded him.

The pilots' mission was simple: patrol the coast in search of enemy submarines—Japanese subs. The flight schedule was tagged as "routine." No Japanese submarines had been sighted in the area and none were expected to be seen during the flight.

"Maybe we'll spot a mermaid," Lieutenant Cody, the flight captain with almost five hundred flying hours to his credit, mused at the patrol assignment.

He recalled with pride the time he piloted the L-8 on his "major contribution" toward winning the war. On April 11, 1942, he had maneuvered the airship over the busy flight deck of the aircraft carrier Hornet as she steamed westward off the California coast. The carrier was in a hurry and had pulled away from the San Francisco dockside before all her cargo had been delivered. After smartly out-maneuvering the trick air current, Cody and his copilot had gently lowered two boxes of special navigational equipment to the waiting Hornet sailors.

A week later, on April 18, the L-8 delivered navigational equipment was put to good use. It had been installed in the sixteen B-25 medium bombers which, led by Lieutenant Colonel James H. Doolittle, took off from the Hornet's flight deck in their history-making bombing raid on Tokyo.

Strange things began to happen almost two hours after the airship took off for patrol duty. The log of the control tower at Naval Air Station, Moffett Field, Alameda, Calif., headquarters of Airship Squadron 32, notes that Lieutenant Cody sent a radio message at 7:50 a.m.: "Investigating suspicious oil slick—stand by."

The airship's position at that time was about five miles east of the Farallon Islands.

Since oil slicks in that area are common, Lieutenant Cody's report caused no excitement at headquarters.

An attempt to make radio contact with the airship was made at 6:05 p.m., according to log entries. The L-8 failed to respond. Alarmed, the air control officer at Alameda ordered two OS2U Kingfisher search planes to investigate.

The airplanes found the ceiling too low, and not wanting to take the chance of colliding with the airship, they decided to stay on top of the clouds.

At 10:45 a.m. someone reported to Moffett Field that an airship had landed at Fort Funston. Two men had disembarked. The airship took off again without the men.

Thirty minutes later, word was received that the L-8 had settled to earth at Daly City. There were no crewmen aboard.

The Navy rushed a salvage party to Daly City and found the ship in fair condition—virtually intact. A bomb was missing but the radio was operative. The classified document portfolio was in order. Rubber life jackets were missing, but the life raft was in place. The motors were stopped, although one throttle was open and the other half-open. Ignition switches were still turned on.

There was no trace of the pilots.

Alarm grew for the safety of Cody and Adams when the Navy learned that they had not landed at Fort Funston. The earlier report had been in error. What actually happened, about a mile from the Fort, was this: The airship drifted in from the Pacific and, descending, slowly struck the beach. Two bathers saw the ship corning down and attempted to seize the handling lines.

When the ship hit the ground a bomb was knocked off giving the craft enough static lift to send it on its way to Daly City, its next stop.

The bathers told Navy investigators that when the L-8 drifted in from the sea there was nobody on board. The engines were stopped and the gondola door was open.

Continuing the inquiry, naval investigators learned that other Navy and Coast Guard vessels had been in the area where Airship L-8 was checking the mysterious oil slick. Boat crewmen told of seeing the L-8 getting ready to make a bombing run on the oil slick, and then suddenly disappear into the overcast. They had not seen the airship again.

A Pan American Airways clipper sighted the airship at 10:30 a.m. and, ten minutes later, one of the aircraft sent out by Moffett air control saw the blimp break through the overcast at 2,000 feet, then descend into it again.

There end the known facts concerning the crew's disappearance. Cody and Adams were declared missing August 16, 1942, and were presumed dead as of August 17, 1943.

What really had happened to Lieutenant Cody and Ensign Adams?

Did a daring enemy submarine eject oil into the sea to attract and trap the patrolling Navy blimp?

Is it possible that a Japanese submarine surfaced and surprised the low-flying airship in the heavy fog?

Could gunners aboard a Japanese submarine have forced the two pilots to jump out of their airship to be taken prisoner?

U.S. Navy investigators discount the submarine theory for two reasons: First, any surfacing submarine would surely have been spotted by the many surface craft operating in the area. Second, no enemy submarines were reported in the area and the classified folder was secure when the blimp landed.

However, since no World War II submarine spotting system was flawless, it never can be certain that an undetected Japanese sub did not cause the disappearance of the two U.S. Navy pilots. However, Japanese war records fail to show that any of their submarines captured the two missing American fliers.

Navy officials say the most logical theory is that the crew's disappearance was accidental and unintentional, that at some time during the flight one of the officers may have leaned out of the gondola, lost his balance, and fallen part way out. The other then rushed to his aid and during the struggle to get back into the gondola both fell from the ship. The open door is regarded as fairly good evidence that they left the ship by that means.

However, the position of the throttles does not verify this theory, for the pilot certainly would not leave one engine full and the other halfway when he went back to pull his companion into the airship.

59

Whatever caused the disappearance of Cody and Adams must have happened fast. The mystery is heightened by the fact that both officers obviously were wearing their life jackets. Had they fallen into the sea, these life jackets would have kept them afloat. But if so, why weren't they spotted and picked up by the many surface craft patrolling the area?

Did Cody and Adams swim or drift ashore? If so, where are they?

If they were drowned, why were their bodies never found?

After twenty-five years the U.S. Navy still is looking for the answer to the riddle of Airship L-8.

THE DAY I DROWNED

Peter Ballbusch
As Told to Dr. R. W. Fischer

I was, I believe, five years old when my brothers decided to give me a swimming lesson in the brook which meandered through a nearby meadow. This brook connected two mill ponds, an upper and a lower one. When water was needed to turn the mill wheel a sluice was opened at the upper pond.

Shortly after my brothers threw me into the swimming hole in the brook someone opened the sluice at the upper pond. A great wall of water came rushing down the brook. It swept me helter-skelter into the lower-mill pond where debris and muck had collected and remained undisturbed for years. As I frantically kicked and struggled, the muck and slime at the bottom of the pond muddied the water, making it difficult for my brothers, who raced downstream after me and dove repeatedly into the pond, to locate me.

And so I went through the strange and painful experience of drowning. It seemed to me that I was being shot from one huge anvil to another, that big sledgehammers were crashing down upon my chest. No doubt this terrible pounding was the exaggerated beating of my tortured heart.

Then suddenly it seemed that I was swept into a glistening spiral tunnel so narrow that it began to squeeze the last bit of air from my agonized lungs. This tunnel ended in a mere pin-point of light but somehow I knew that I had to squeeze through this tiny opening. It was a painful and frightening experience. I thought my heart would be squeezed right out of my mouth but finally I slipped through the opening and was released from all pain and pressure.

I found myself floating in a strange stream which wended upward into infinity This river carried me along and its water and space and the stars seemed to emit a soothing music, which penetrated my innermost being. It was incredibly beautiful and filled me with bliss and peace.

When I opened my eyes, I saw that the strange river was filled with people of all races and ages; men, women and children drifted along and were carried up toward the stars along with me. They all had their eyes closed and seemed to be listening to the soothing music as I had listened. I wondered with my five-year-old mind if they had drowned, too, and I wondered also where the river would take us.

As we drifted along I saw that the river reached a far-flung shore where people stood waiting in groups, like welcoming parties. The water eddied onto beaches, into coves and nooks and crannies. Hands reached out to pull some of the drifters out of the river. The waiting people hugged and kissed them as if they had come home from a long and dangerous voyage.

While I watched this I thought of my mother, who had died the year before, and I began to wonder if she waited somewhere for me. As I thought about this the river carried me to a ledge where a group of people seemed to be waving at me. I recognized my grandfather and grandmother and some aunts and uncles I had seen pictured in the family album. And right in front of everybody stood my mother! She was all dressed up and she smiled and waved at me. The water carried me close to the ledge where she stood and she knelt down and reached her hand out to me. But I could not reach her. As she leaned forward a black cross slipped out of her blouse and hung on a thin silver chain right in front of my eyes. I was almost blinded by the sparkle of seven stars which flashed from the dark background of the cross, and I wondered what made them shine.

I almost touched Mother's hand; then I suddenly felt myself being pulled away. I seemed to sink into a whirlpool and my mother smiled sadly as she watched me being sucked rapidly down. She became smaller and smaller until her figure was a mere dot, and then she vanished while a roar filled my ears and the whirlpool forced my chest to heave convulsively.

Next I was aware of vomiting the water which the attending fire brigade kept pressing out of me. I learned later they had worked for half an hour to bring me back to life. I was finally carried home and put to bed. One of my sisters fed me a glass of warm milk.

When my father came into the room to ask me how I felt. I told him I had seen Mother. Father listened to my story with an indulgent smile until I came to the incident of the black cross with its seven flashing stars. Then he turned abruptly and left the room.

Not until years later did I learn what had upset Father.

At the time of Mother's death, all of us children were sent to an aunt three railroad hours away from home. Father did not want us to witness the agony of Mother's passing. Mother died three days before her birthday but Father had already bought her birthday present. It was a beautiful black onyx cross with seven silver stars on it. After Mother's death when she was laid out in her coffin, Father told me, he had slipped the black cross into her folded hands and she had been buried with it.

No one had known this except Father, and he couldn't ever understand how I came to know about the cross, unless I really had seen it and Mother somewhere in another world beyond that river.

How else can this be explained?

FOUND—THE WITCHES' SALVE

Jack Dunning

With aching leg muscles I pedaled my bicycle slowly up the long gradual incline of the Berg Strasse, the lovely mountain road that stretches from Wieslock to Darmstadt in southwestern Germany. I was on my way to visit a man who had, only a short time before, experienced a genuine Witches' Sabbath.

It was hard to reconcile the stream of modern cars, trucks and busses along the busy highway with a medieval adventure of this type.

Yet the man I was going to see is as modern as the new cars rolling along the asphalt. Full professor at Gottingen, one of Germany's great universities, author of books and one of Europe's foremost authorities on occultism, Dr. Erich-Will Peuckert is no wild-eyed wizard mixing bat's blood and toads in an iron caldron. He is a highly trained, scientifically minded scientist in his field. What he had to say was not the irresponsible rantings of a sensation-seeker but the considered findings of a qualified and respected academician.

Dr. Peuckert's house is as unlike a wizard's lair as could be imagined. It resembles one of the better houses to be found almost anywhere in the United States suburbs. Dr. Peuckert himself proved to be reassuringly un-wizardlike, as well as friendly and cooperative.

Shaking his hand, I was struck by the realization that had his experience taken place only a few hundred years before, he almost certainly would have been burned at the stake for it.

For Dr. Peuckert is one of probably only two living persons ever to have attended a real Witches' Sabbath.

The story actually begins nearly forty years ago when Dr. Peuckert first took up the study of occult phenomena. In his study of the ancient books and manuscripts of the Middle Ages he kept running into all kinds of magical recipes and formulas. A scientist of insatiable curiosity, Dr. Peuckert personally tested about sixty such formulas over the years.

As a simple example, he describes the medieval formula for taming a savage dog. The directions call for the trainer to feed the dog a piece of bread he had carried in his armpit for an entire day. The manuscript advises that this procedure will make the dog friendly with the donor.

Dr. Peuckert tried the formula and found that it works. He explains that the bread absorbs the personal body scent of the trainer. Dogs depend largely upon scent for identification and attitude and by eating the bread they accept the person's personal scent and with it the person.

Today we understand how this works because we understand something about the behavior and motivation of animals. But during the Middle Ages such a procedure was regarded as magic.

The same kind of process also works between human beings, but since it involves humans, and since somehow the unconscious mind may be implicated, it appears to be much closer to magic than the dog training formula.

By using human bodily extracts, Dr. Peuckert has been able to induce a "physical and subconscious affinity" between male and female test subjects. Again, the formula, though modified, came from medieval books on witchcraft.

Female students at the University of Gottingen were used as test subjects in the experiments. Dr. Peuckert hastens to point out that the tests were "scientific and carried out with all the necessary safeguards."

First, extracts of skin oils or saliva were obtained from unknown young men. These extracts were chemically purified and fortified, then injected into candies and fruit.

The girl test subjects who ate the fruit showed an "irresistible and otherwise inexplicable determination" to meet the person from whom the extracts had been prepared and they were able to pick the man out of a group of people.

This and similar research reports were given sensational treatment in the European Press, and Dr. Peuckert was greatly upset by the news stories. As a result he is quite reticent about what he is willing to report for publication on these subjects. Shortly after I saw him he stopped giving interviews altogether.

Most sensational of Dr. Peuckert's findings and experiences, however, were those involving the "witches' salve."

Dr. Peuckert discovered the formula in a book called *Magia Naturalis,* written by Johannes Baptista Porta in 1588. It is a rare book, written in archaic Latin, nearly impossible to obtain and difficult to read. To translate it properly, one must be not only a scholar in Medieval Latin but a research specialist in alchemy and witchcraft.

Dr. Peuckert is careful not to reveal the formula, but the salve for the most part is made from plants which are readily available, though extremely dangerous.

Included are thornapple, a bushy plant with small apple-like fruit covered with spines. Thornapple is common over most of the United States and Europe and bears the Latin name *Datura Stramortium*. Another ingredient is henbane *(Hyoscyamus Niger)*, a low, flowering plant which is highly poisonous and gets its name from the fact that chickens often die from eating it. A third ingredient is deadly nightshade *(Atropa Belladonna)*, a poisonous woodland plant which contains *atropin*, a drug affecting the heart and eyes. This too is widely distributed, and like the others grows wild. Wild celery and parsley are also in the salve.

The original magical instructions call for the fat of an unbaptized infant. Dr. Peuckert used ordinary lard from a supermarket—the pigs that produced it being, presumably, unbaptized.

Dr. Peuckert warns that any attempt to reproduce the salve without complete knowledge of the ingredients and their proportions would probably result at best in a stay in the hospital and at worst in a speedy trip to the morgue.

As a good scientist, Dr. Peuckert did not hesitate to test the salve on himself. And, also as a good scientist, he needed a control in order that his observations might be objectively and subjectively verified.

He chose as his companion for the experiment an attorney friend whose name he refuses to reveal and who knew nothing whatever about witchcraft prior to the experiment, or about the effects the salve might produce.

And so, at six o'clock one evening, Dr. Peuckert and his friend retired to a private room. Following the directions in *Magia Naturalis* they applied the salve to their foreheads and armpits.

Within a few minutes both fell into a deep, trance-like sleep which lasted for twenty hours. They awoke with all the symptoms of a vicious hangover. Their mouths were dry, their throats hurt, they had blinding headaches. But they had lived through that wildest and most depraved of all debauches—the Witches' Sabbath!

What was it like?

Dr. Peuckert is reticent in his description. He had visions of horribly distorted human faces. He had a feeling of flying for miles through the air. His flight was, from time to time, interrupted by dizzying swoops and plunges. He landed on a mountaintop.

Finally came the celebration of the Sabbath itself, with wild orgies and grotesque debauchery, with voluptuous young ladies playing a prominent part. Beings with the appearance of monsters and demons joined in the erotic activities. They indulged in perverted sex practices and they paid homage to the Devil.

Despite his hangover, Dr. Peuckert remained a scientist.

His first act on returning to consciousness was to write a complete, detailed report of his experiences and to obtain a similar document from his friend before they compared notes.

Details on these notes cannot be published here, but when Dr. Peuckert compared his report with that of his attorney friend he was momentarily speechless. The reports were virtually identical! Except for differences in terminology and expression, both men described the same experiences.

Even more significant, as far as Dr. Peuckert's scientific research was concerned, both reports written by these professional men in the year 1960 tallied in every detail with the recorded statements of accused witches who had died at the stake during the witchcraft trials of the Middle Ages!

This was the answer Dr. Peuckert had been seeking. He knew now that witches' tales of olden times were not mere products of imagination or insanity but factual reports. Men and women had known the secret of the salve and had used it.

The witches really had celebrated their diabolical Sabbath and, although their experiences had not been physical ones, they believed they had been. Dr. Peuckert, assumes that the witches of the Middle Ages did not differentiate the trance state from reality, just as small children often do not separate their dreams from incidents which occur during their waking hours.

No wonder the witches had confessed so often and in such detail. Many of them must have gone to their deaths sincerely believing they stood guilty as charged!

Further evidence substantiating Dr. Peuckert's theories explains why witchcraft first emerged in Germany during the Middle Ages. It was at this time that the plants necessary to prepare the drug were introduced into northern Europe. The secrets of the salve and its use are believed to have been brought to Germany by roving bands of gypsies. The knowledge was disseminated by groups of women whose female secret societies represented the vestiges of an older matriarchal culture that Dr. Peuckert believes had its roots in the south of France but may have been spread over a much wider area.

Regardless of the findings, many questions are left unanswered in this report.

Why, for instance, does every person using the salve dream the identical dream?

How can a drug invariably produce such complicated visual and tactile sensations?

Can a person really dream of something for which there was no precedent in his mind?

Dr. Peuckert suggests that the salve may work, for example, like the effect of the drug *atropin*, which invariably causes dilation of the pupil of the eye. He regards the narcotic action of the salve as a similar, purely chemical reaction on the brain which, in all cases, leads to the same impressions.

But is this a complete, satisfactory explanation of the visions, the flying sensations, the sexual orgies? It seems to me to be inadequate—or at the minimum it seems to me to be open to argument.

It has been suggested that the unchanging manifestations of the drug may be explained by something lying buried in the human mind itself.

Can it stimulate a specific segment of racial memory? And if so, memory of what? Of times when men flew? Of human orgies with nonhumans? Or with masked humans?

Or are these experiences, after all, merely symbolic expressions or mechanistic hallucinations, as the psychologists have always believed?

It was well past two in the morning when I left Dr. Peuckert's home. On my left rose the conifer clad slopes of the mountains—the Odenwald—forest of the Teutonic god Odin. And on the mountain crests crouched ancient ruins. In such a place, at such a time, it seemed to me anything might happen.

THE LITTLE MAN WHO WAS SOMETIMES THERE

McMichael Bean
As Told to A. L. Lloyd

I first saw the little old man in 1880. I was working on the Circle J ranch near Vinita, Indian Territory, now in the state of Oklahoma. One morning I was walking across a small horse pasture to catch my favorite horse and there he was, walking by my side.

He appeared to be about sixty-five years old, with long graying beard, wearing a shabby brown suit, worn shoes, and a crushed hat. He was about four and one-half feet tall. I spoke to him but he seemed not to hear. I raised my voice and spoke again. He made no answer and I figured he was stone deaf.

As I walked up to put a bridle on my horse I looked around and there was no little man in sight. I often had heard of people seeing appearing and disappearing ghosts, so I decided the little old man was one of that kind. After that I would often see him walking at my side, or if I was riding a horse I would see him walking ahead of me.

After he had come around a few times I decided to consult an old Cherokee woman who lived in the White Oak vicinity, five or six miles away. I had heard she would give advice and information on different subjects and would take no pay, but would accept a gift or present. So I bought a supply of smoking tobacco and rode out to her two-room log cabin.

I introduced myself and told her of my experiences with the little old man. She gazed out the little cabin window with a far-away look in her eyes for about a minute, then said, "Mr. Bean, that little old man is your guardian angel. When he appears going your way, well and good; but if you meet him or see him coming toward you, turn back, for there is danger ahead."

Now, there was a ranch about thirty miles southwest of the Circle J known as the Bar-K-Bar (-K-), and we had heard that Mr. Kimball was selling some of his surplus cattle. A few days after my visit to the old Indian woman Mr. Jordan, our boss and owner of the Circle J, came to me and said, "Mac, I want you to ride down to the -K-, look their cattle over, and if you find any worth buying I will authorize you to deal for twenty-five head. Kimball will furnish two boys to help you drive the cattle here."

This was about mid-April. The weather was warm and grass was beginning to show on the prairies and low places. I started at dawn and a half mile from the -K-, out of nowhere, appeared the little old man walking ahead of me. I thought of the old Indian woman's words, "well and good."

Early next morning we rode out among the -K- herds and I began selecting what I thought were good buys. As picked out an animal, the -K- boys would cut it out of the herd and drive it to a large corral. By noon I had the twenty-five head corralled.

While selecting the twenty-five head I noticed over in the horse pasture a good looking, slim-built black horse that seemed to be of racing stock. I asked some of the boys who owned that horse. They told me a fellow known as Slim owned him.

Good cow ponies could be bought at that time for $25 to $35, but Slim wanted $50 for Blackie, as he intended to train him for racing, as did I, if I could buy him. After haggling some over the price I did buy Blackie.

When I had the time, mostly on Sundays, I began training Blackie on a one-mile straight track. I gradually lengthened the distance till Blackie could run the mile without too much effort. By fall Blackie had beaten every so-called race horse in the community.

Several miles east of the Circle J the Rankin brothers operated a ranch. They owned a horse that had outrun every horse in their community and when they heard about Blackie they came over on a Sunday and challenged me and Blackie to a race, offering to put up $100 on their horse, Red.

The horses ran the race with Blackie winning by three lengths.

Here is where my troubles began. And the little old man with the shabby clothes saved my life.

I had heard that the Rankins had a shady reputation for acquiring property by illegal methods. After the race they immediately offered me their horse and $100 for Blackie. Of course, I refused. They went away disgruntled and angry because Blackie had beaten their horse and I had refused to deal with them. They came over a couple of times later and the last time they came I became suspicious of them. I bought two padlocks, and locked one end of a chain around Blackie's neck and the other end around a log of the corn crib.

70

One day soon after that, one of the Rankins came over and, after arguing for half an hour, he left saying, "If you don't deal with us you might wish you had. We will be back tomorrow."

That left me with something to ponder over. I decided they were going to get Blackie by hook or crook. The next day they came over and raised their offer by $25. I decided to deal, as $125 and their horse was a fair offer, and if I still refused I might find Blackie dead or stolen. This was in October when, after a light frost or two, foliage had begun to wither and die.

Occasionally I heard that Blackie had developed into a speedy race horse and was winning all through the winter. The next spring, about the middle of April, the Rankin boys rode over and demanded to know what kind of disease Blackie had. They said they found him dead that morning. I told them they knew as well as I did that nothing was wrong with Blackie when we made the deal, that if there had been he could not have won all those races.

I rode over to the Rankin place and found Blackie. He was swollen and greenish fluid was dripping from his nostrils. I knew immediately what had caused his death. When the Rankins rode up a minute later I said, "Boys, Blackie has eaten the deadly buckeye and that is the cause of his death."

"No!" they answered in unison. "Stock in this country know buckeye and won't touch it."

I tried to explain to them that Blackie was raised on the plains and did not know buckeye, and buckeye is the first plant or bush to put out tiny green buds and leaves in early spring. Blackie, being eager for green stuff after a winter of dry feed, ate a lot of those buds and leaves, and it kills an animal in eight to ten hours.

The Rankins wouldn't have it that way. They insisted on the return of Red and the $125. I said no, and I walked along the edge of the timber and pointed out to them where Blackie had nipped off buds and leaves and showed them his tracks, clearly visible near the buckeye bushes.

"Well, are you going to return Red and $125?" they insisted.

"No," I replied, "and no law compels anyone to return money and stock after six months in a case like this." They rode away saying, "You'll wish you had."

The next Friday night there was to be a dance at a large farmhouse about five miles away. I got off work about four o'clock and began fixing up to go to the dance.

I started out about sundown and a half mile from the ranch I looked up and who should I see but the little old man coming down the road *toward me.* I stopped my horse and sat there watching for some sign from the little man but he seemed not to see me and within thirty yards of me he just disappeared.

I sure did want to go to the dance but, remembering the old Indian woman's words, I regretfully turned back to the ranch.

The next morning a neighbor boy came riding by and stopped at the corral where I was repairing some harness. "How was the dance," I asked him, as I knew he'd gone. "Had a good time. But it was a good thing for you that you wasn't there."

"Why?" I asked.

"Because the Rankins were there with pistols on, looking for you to kill you," he said.

As I didn't want to kill anyone, or to be killed myself, I settled up my accounts with Mr. Jordan and left for the old home place down in what is now Adair County, Okla., far to the south. I had been engaged for nearly a year and I figured I had enough to start married life on. So I married and settled down.

And I never saw the little man in the shabby brown suit again.

THE LEGEND OF THE BLACK CHRIST OF PORTO BELLO

Rayn Shawk

Many Indian slaves died during the early days of the conquistadors. At least one died with a curse on his lips.

In a forgotten village in Peru a talented young man had finished carving a life-size image of his new Savior, a Savior who would help his people as He had helped others; a Savior who promised deliverance. The young Indian, carving in secrecy for over a year, had shaped an ebony log into the image of Christ. As he carved he dreamed of the day when he could present the statue to the village priest, a statue that would bring deliverance from the cruel taskmasters with their gold lust. The god of the white men, now the god of the Indians also, was powerful. His son, the Savior, was powerful, too. Surely He would take notice of the honor the people accorded His image and come to their aid.

The wood-carver polished the great figure for the last time. He was about to have it carried to the priest when the Spanish captain, the governor of the village, came upon him and his work. The tall Spaniard looked with surprise at the black figure. This would make an excellent gift for the church in Castile, perhaps even Madrid! A ship was being loaded at the very moment, to sail with the next tide. Gold, slaves, fine woods, and many rare and valuable things from the New World were going on the long trip to Spain, he insisted, adding that this statue would round out the long list of wonderful gifts.

The captain, without a word to the young artist, ordered the statue carried to the ship and stowed in the hold. The Indian leaped before the startled captain. No! The statue would remain here in the village church! The statue would be the Savior of the Indians!

Never had one of these savages dared speak up to a soldier of Spain. The captain was outraged, insulted. In one motion he drew his blade and ran it through the proud man's young body. The Indian collapsed at the feet of his Christ.

According to legend, as the young slave fell the statue suddenly changed.

73

It changed from a gentle, beatific Christ to a strange, bent, bloody and belabored Christ, a Christ who had seen the horrors of man; a Christ on his way to Golgotha. The eyes, once gentle and filled with love, were now filled with horror. The onyx pupils, encircled with mother-of-pearl, now stare out at a world of cruelty and fear.

As the Indian lay dying he turned his eyes to the captain, and in his own tongue, he called to his old gods. They must never allow his new Savior to leave his people, never let his Christ serve the Spanish masters.

The body of the carver was dragged away and the statue carried to the hold of the ship. Within hours it was under way to Panama City. There the ship would be unloaded, and the cargo would be carried across the isthmus on the newly-built highway, the Camino Real, to Porto Bello. There it would be loaded onto another ship and sail to Spain. All went well for the expedition until the time to set sail for Spain. The ship had been refitted for the voyage after being battered almost to pieces in a savage Caribbean hurricane. It had a new, untried crew; most of the men were soldiers going home to Spain, pressed into service as sailors.

Perhaps the untrained crew was responsible, perhaps the workmanship during the refitting had been poor, perhaps it was the Indian wood-carver's curse; at any rate, just as the ship was about to clear the harbor a sudden wind spun the vessel around, tore the big sail loose, and snapped the main mast. The heavy timber and canvas thundered to the deck, bringing down with it the men who had been working in the rigging.

The ship was towed back to the dock. Work began at once to replace the mast. In a matter of days the ship was again ready for the long voyage. Again disaster struck! A seam opened in the hull of the vessel; the hold filled with water, and the ship settled in twenty feet of water.

For three weeks, master and slave labored side by side to clear the harbor. Finally the ship was once again secured to the stone dock. The hold was emptied, cargo washed and dried in the sun, the entire ship gone over, scrubbed, cleaned, recaulked. Once more the gifts for Spain were loaded. Once more the ship was ready. Then came more trouble!

A strange sickness affected only the white-skinned Spaniards. The Indians were untouched, while the conquistadors went down like flies. It was not a killing disease, but men were driven nearly to suicide to escape the agony that wracked their bodies.

Both the governor and the ship's captain were anxious to get the ship under way to Spain. It had been delayed too long already. As a last resort it was decided to gather as many able crewmen as possible and supplement the ranks with Indian slaves. When a complete crew was assembled the Indians outnumbered the sailors more than three to one.

The captain was worried. These Indians had been at sea on short trips, of course, but no one ever had dared an ocean crossing with a crew like the one now assembled.

Nevertheless, the captain ordered the ship cast off.

The Indians were frightened of the long voyage. They hung in the rigging and chanted, prayed, and wept. Slowly the ungainly vessel crossed the half mile of calm water to the mouth of the harbor. Then suddenly the sky darkened, a vicious wind arose, rain fell in sheets. The Indians, perhaps in superstitious panic, leaped over the side, leaving the handful of Spanish sailors to handle the heaving vessel.

In less than ten minutes the sudden storm was over. The ship rested once again on the harbor bottom!

Four weeks later the captain saw the "Black Christ" emerge from the hold of his ship. He had thought many times during the last month of the story of the curse told by the porters who brought the cargo over the isthmus; the curse that said the statue would never leave the Indian people. The captain made up his mind! Leaping from the quarterdeck he ran to the gangplank.

"That cursed thing stays!" he shouted pointing at the statue.

Silence fell over the waterfront. Sacrilege! He suddenly realized what he had said; what he had done. It was too late to take back his words ... he stood firm. Eternal damnation or not, that statue would not board his ship again.

The governor sent for him. He spoke to the priests. The officers of the garrison tried to reason with him. Word had been sent ahead that the statue was coming. If it was deemed worthy it might go to Rome. He had to take it along or face possible execution.

He stood firm ... execution, damnation, nothing could change his mind. On October 23 of a long forgotten year the unknown captain once again set sail. Hundreds watched along the waterfront. The "Black Christ" stood where it had been unloaded. The ship sailed out of the harbor and out of sight. Silence held for perhaps half an hour. Then one of the Indian slaves let out a shout. He and several of his fellows laid hold of the statue and, chanting, they lifted the heavy figure to their shoulders and began a procession through the town. They had gotten a Savior; from now on their burden would be a little lighter. The Savior of a little village in a remote section of Peru now had become the "Black Christ" of Porto Bello.

At one time the pirate Morgan nearly destroyed the city of Porto Bello.

Every building save the harbor fortress and the church of the "Black Christ" was leveled. The records that told in detail the story of the coming of the statue were destroyed, leaving only the legend. During the intervening four hundred and fifty years some things have been forgotten. What was the name of the captain who first found the statue and murdered the young slave? What was the name of the unlucky ship that tried to carry the image to Spain? Who was her captain?

But the important fact is that the statue is still in Porto Bello; it is still the Savior of the descendants of the Indian slaves who first carried the "Black Christ" through the streets on their shoulders.

This first procession is re-enacted every year.

Through the long years and many processions the statue has acquired a cross to carry and a crown of thorns to wear on its bloody brow. Now a secondary figure holds the lower end of the cross. Some say this figure represents the brave captain who ordered the statue off his ship. He is depicted as helping the "Black Christ" carry the burdens of the Indians of Porto Bello. Both figures now are clothed in rich purple robes. They stand on a heavy mahogany platform. Lighted candles surround them.

At festival time, every October 23, the statue's robes are hung with medals containing prayers and wishes to be granted. It is surrounded with flowers and clouds of incense. The church is filled with chanting. And the whole affair, Christ, cross, flowers, and candles, finally is lifted onto the shoulders of about sixty strong men and carried from the church, to be paraded through the town. The celebrants walk with a hopping three-forward-and two-backward step, accompanied by pipes and tomtoms.

Promptly at eight o'clock the procession leaves the church. Promptly at eight o'clock the rain ceases. The rain, which falls almost continuously at this time of year in Porto Bello, either in a fine mist or in torrents, ceases abruptly as the statue emerges from the church door. Never in the more than four hundred and fifty year history of the festival has rain touched the Black Christ.

In front of the church hundreds of people stand: tourists, servicemen from near-by bases in the Canal Zone, Indians, and here and there a robed figure. The robed ones are penitents, who have asked that a prayer or wish be granted. Throughout the year prayers and wishes are written on a piece of paper, affixed to a medal and hung on the robes of the "Black Christ." If the prayer is answered or the wish granted the beseecher does a promised penance. Such penance often takes the form of walking on bare feet and wearing purple robes until the next festival. However, more severe penances are in order if the prayer or wish is especially important.

One young boy, whose mother lay on her deathbed and was believed cured as the result of a prayer to the "Black Christ," wore a crown of real thorns and carried a heavy wooden cross for the two months remaining until the next festival.

An old fruit vendor tells the story of a man whose son was lost in the jungle. He prayed to the "Black Christ" for his son's return. When the boy walked out of the jungle several days later, well and unharmed, the old man had his hands nailed to the arms of a cross and carried it thus for several weeks.

These people may seem to be fanatics in their worship of their Savior, but perhaps they are justified. Discounting all the tales of miraculous cures and impossible wishes granted, one has still to consider the phenomenon of the rain, the constant, chill rain that falls on Porto Bello in October.

As you stand before that old, old church in the candlelit darkness, waiting, shivering, time seems to fall away. When the church door opens the almost pagan sound of the pipes and drums filters out into the night. Then the procession appears. The statue, lurching back and forth high in the air, leaves the shelter of the church ... and instantly the rain stops. The stars break through the scattering clouds as if to watch and the yellow tropical moon shines down on the blood-stained face of the "Black Christ" of Porto Bello.

DEATH WEARS JOHNNY'S FACE

Etna Elliot

In Portland, Ore., on the very hot summer night of August 9, 1918, on the eve of my wedding day, my parents, my young brother, and I had just returned from the home of my aunt and uncle, who lived on the east side of the city, where my marriage was to take place the following day. We were all tired but happy.

I was just too excited to sleep. I was lying on the bed, relaxing, just gazing off into space without even thinking, when suddenly I became conscious of someone walking through my open door.

To see my fiancé walk slowly through the door and cross the room to the foot of my bed was so startling that I sat right up in bed. I started to speak his name, when the terrible expression on his face froze the words in my throat. I never have seen such sadness stamped upon a face. He looked like wax; his face was so strained and drawn that I thought he was going to cry. As he reached out his hand to me I screamed, "Johnny, Johnny, are you all right?"

At that he seemed to sag and I thought he might fall, but he straightened up and looked behind him, as if he were looking at someone near the door of my room. Then he stooped as if to touch me but suddenly turned and walked back through my door into the hallway. He looked back at me with that agonized look of sadness still on his face, then disappeared into the darkness.

I was crying and calling his name as I ran through the darkness of the hallway almost into the arms of my father, who had heard me call out the first time and was hurrying to my room. Both my parents tried to quiet me by insisting that I had been dreaming. But I knew I had not been asleep. I knew I had seen Johnny. And I knew that something was wrong.

My mother made me drink hot milk and finally got me quiet and back in my bed. They both stayed in my room until I fell asleep.

It was just breaking day when the shrill ringing of the telephone in the hallway brought me wide awake. As I stumbled toward the phone I heard my father say, "No! No! There must be some mistake! Are you sure? Oh! My God, where? Yes, I'll be right there."

As he turned from the telephone Father pulled my head over on his chest and stroked my hair, saying, "You were right. You were right. Johnny was here."

I just stared at Father. I couldn't seem to understand what lie was saying. But Mother understood, for she ran to their room crying wildly. Only then did the truth begin to seep into my shocked mind: Johnny was dead! He had come to tell me goodbye. That's why he was so sad, why his face was filled with terror, why he was so white and why he was looking behind him. Someone was waiting to take him—where? Where would they take him?

My father put me to bed where I stayed for many a day.

We learned later that Johnny had been driving through from Seattle, Wash., with a buddy of his, expecting to be at my aunt's and uncle's home early in the morning on our wedding day.

In 1918 the roads between Portland and Seattle were nothing but cow trails and their car had struck a large boulder that had fallen into the road, throwing them over a cliff. Johnny was pinned under the car and when they finally pulled him from the wreckage, he was dead.

All the beautiful wedding gifts were returned. My lovely bridal dress was wrapped in tissue and carefully put away. Everything was put out of my sight. My solicitous parents thought that with no sign of a wedding I might turn to other thoughts. Nothing eased the pain of knowing that I would never see Johnny again. But about this I was wrong. For I did see Johnny again and again. And it always meant death to me when he came.

About ten months from the time Johnny was killed, on June 14, 1919, my friend Florence and I were walking across the Morrison Street Bridge one evening, enjoying the cool breeze of the Willamette River when I again saw Johnny. He was walking rapidly toward us as if in a great hurry. I stopped dead in my tracks, Florence stopped a few steps ahead of me and, looking back, said, "Etna, what is it?"

Johnny walked to within a few feet of me. His face was shadowed and drawn as he looked down into my face.

Florence came back and took hold of my arms. Over her shoulder I saw Johnny disappear into the shadows. As she shook me I began to cry, telling her I had seen Johnny.

"Oh! Didn't you see him, Florence?" I sobbed. "He stood right there."

Florence led me gently but firmly to the end of the bridge where she called a cab and got me home as quickly as possible. Once there we found that my grandfather had had a stroke and had died before they could get him to the hospital. My parents had been trying to locate me.

Johnny had found me first. He had come to tell me of my grandfather's death.

After the funeral of my beloved grandfather, I was numb with grief. My parents, fearing for my health, sent me to California to visit an aunt and uncle there, and through my young cousin, I met a fine young man, fell in love, and was married the following summer.

As time passed the memory of Johnny became dim. I now had three lovely children and was a busy, happy young mother. We had our own home in Portland just a few miles from my parents and my brother, now also married and with a family of his own.

However, I was not to forget Johnny! September 26, 1931, was hot, and in the evening my husband and I took the children and drove out Washington Street to the beautiful, cool park there in the foothills. We were sitting on the lawn watching the children play. It was dark by this time and the children played close to us. Suddenly my little son stopped right at my feet and looked up at someone. I followed his gaze and there was Johnny! I jumped to my feet and screamed.

It had been twelve years since I last had seen Johnny. I was frozen with fear, for I knew death was near me or mine. We rushed to our car and drove at once to my parents' home where our worst fears were realized. An ambulance, a police car and our family doctor's large sedan stood before the house. I was met by my father. Together, he and the doctor told me as gently as possible that my mother had died of a heart attack twenty minutes before.

Johnny had found me again! Why did he always come to tell me of the death of a loved one? Now I lived in complete terror of seeing Johnny again. I prayed that he would never come to me again, and I thought this prayer was answered, for I did not see Johnny again for the next twelve years.

Our children were all growing up. Our oldest son finished school and joined the United States Marines and soon was sent overseas. Like all mothers, I was frightened but I tried to trust in God. Many years ago I had placed my children in his keeping.

Then in the early morning of November 5, 1943, I awoke from a horrible dream. I had seen my son trying to come to me down a long flight of stairs. Both of his legs were off just below the hips and blood was running down the steps ahead of him. He was sobbing and calling, "Mother, Mother." And I was trying to climb those stairs to go to him, but somehow I couldn't seem to get up those steps that were slippery with blood. My legs had no strength and I kept falling back as my son called me through his sobs.

I awoke in a cold sweat, shaking with terror, so sick I could hardly stand on my feet as I climbed slowly from bed, put on my robe, and walked the floor for hours, from room to room, with my teeth chattering as from a chill. It was just breaking day when I walked into the living room and up to the front window in time to see a man crossing our lawn. Without even thinking I rushed across the room, threw open the door, and there was Johnny! I grabbed the door jamb for support and I guess I screamed, for my husband was there, trying to get my clutching hands loose from the jamb and I could still see Johnny as he reached out to me, and I heard myself screaming "Johnny, Johnny" over and over.

Later I tried to tell my husband about my terrible dream, and he knew that Johnny had been there although he had not seen him, and he began to tremble. He was afraid also, for he had learned what Johnny's visits meant to us. We were both positive that our son was dead.

Not until the third day after Johnny's visit did word come from the war department informing us that our son had died in the service of his country.

This was the same boy who, at the age of six, saw Johnny himself. He was the only one besides myself who ever did see Johnny.

Now, more than sixteen years after the death of our son, our life is shadowed with sadness and fear. I try to overcome this fear, but I cannot help wondering when I will see Johnny again.

Why does he come only with death? Why hasn't he let me see him at other times? Why does he come at all? What does it all mean? Where is Johnny? He has never grown old. In 1943 he was the same young boy that I was to have married twenty-five years before, while I have grown old with worry, grief and fear.

I know Johnny will come back! But, why?

CROSS-COUNTRY DEMONSTRATION OF ESP

Peter Ballbusch

In this analytical time, millions are being spent to discover the hidden potentials of the human mind. Laboratories and research departments are using drugs, psychotherapy and hypnosis to explore men's minds.

Two researchers, well aware of present progress in this field, decided to try an extrasensory experiment across a distance of 2,200 miles. Dr. Robert G. Chaney of the Astara Foundation in Los Angeles, Calif., and Rev. Austin Wallace, at that time associated with the Spiritual Episcopal Church of Eaton Rapids, Mich., knew that the experiment might attract criticism; however, they accepted the challenge of the untried.

The stage was set with a special telephone connection between the two churches and then, on the memorable Sunday of April 13, 1958, both men prepared to project their awareness clear across the country into the church of their fellow pastor.

When we asked Dr. Chaney how he achieved this attunement he explained that his focused projection demanded extreme concentration, which at times was exhausting, but that once he became dimly aware of the interior of the church in Eaton Rapids, his psychic perception increased steadily. Finally, he reached a stage of contact in which he was able to tell the faraway persons to whom he gave messages on which side of the church they were seated.

Reverend Wallace, who returned Dr. Chaney's demonstration, said also that the initial attunement was exhausting, but he, too, gave accurate descriptions of details at Astara which no one could have communicated to him.

The telephones in each church were connected with loudspeakers so that the entire audience could hear the relayed messages clearly.

By analyzing a few of the messages given, and by separating the "unknowable" from the "knowable," we can get a good idea of the accuracy of this cross-country mind projection.

A Mrs. Myrna L. Treacher was contacted by Dr. Chaney and told that she was seated in the choir on the left side of the church, and that her daughters were seated in the nave below the right side. Dr. Chaney stated over the long-distance telephone that he had a feeling that a great similarity existed between the two girls and he asked if they were identical twins. All this was true, but Mrs. Treacher was even more astounded when a question which had occupied her mind for some time was suddenly answered by Dr. Chaney.

A skeptic might suggest that both the seating and the description of the girls as twins were "knowable" since this information could have been relayed to Dr. Chaney in Los Angeles. However, there had been a change in the seating arrangement shortly before the message came through which served to make this an "unknowable," and, of course, the answering of an unstated question in Mrs. Treacher's mind was certainly "unknowable."

Robert and Frances Harris were told where they were seated, and they received a message from their brother-in-law who had just passed on. Few persons even in Eaton Rapids knew about his death and Mr. and Mrs. Harris wondered how Dr. Chaney picked up this information 2,000 miles away. His description of the deceased was as accurate as if he were watching him across his desk. Again one might argue that the seating was "knowable" since no change had taken place in this case, but the death of the brother-in-law and his description were "unknowable" to Dr. Chaney.

Mrs. Inez Michels was contacted by Dr. Chaney and given details concerning a property settlement. Even the names of the persons involved were given. She was advised as to who could handle the case properly, and what pleased Mrs. Michels most was a detail revealed by her deceased husband that seemed to prove that Dr. Chaney had made contact with her mate.

Since Mrs. Michels had told no one about the property settlement, and Dr. Chaney had no normal way of getting the detail the deceased husband revealed, both these items were "unknowables."

In this manner fourteen members of the Eaton Rapids church received messages from Dr. Chaney. All of them were convinced of the authenticity of the contact and amazed that Dr. Chaney had been able to journey mentally and psychically from California to Michigan.

Rev. Austin Wallace contacted a dozen members of Astara and astonished them with his accuracy and wealth of detail. He described a large vase of red and white flowers standing to the right of the pulpit in Los Angeles. He mentioned that the donor had intended them to be pink in honor of the birthday of her deceased cousin. These things were true.

I have selected a specific message from among the many which Reverend Wallace gave, since it contains an entire series of "unknowables" and was addressed to a person who never before had attended a Sunday service at Astara.

Oliver Hasz recently had moved to California and entered the City College of Engineering. A few weeks before his Sunday visit to Astara his brother, Albert, had been killed in an automobile accident. Oliver was restless and unsettled and wondered if his move to California had been a wise one, and if electrical engineering really would provide him with a satisfying, lucrative livelihood.

This Sunday, as he sat among the many persons participating in the experiment, he had just written the name of his deceased brother on a slip of paper when Reverend Wallace's voice, over the loudspeaker, said, "This is a message for Oliver Hasz to whom his brother Albert sends greetings. Albert approves wholly of your plans for the future. The move west was a wise one, as it will bring wonderful development along spiritual lines. Albert tells me that he is going to do his best to help you."

Oliver Hasz listened spellbound, still holding the slip of paper on which he had written his brother's name. How could a man 2,200 miles away both read his mind and bring him this message from his deceased brother?

You can readily see that Oliver Hasz's message is "unknowable." Being a newcomer to California and to Astara, neither his name nor his plans were known. His brother's presence in the spirit realm, plus his given name, all are "unknowables."

In interviewing some of the participants in this cross-country demonstration I asked them to explain these phenomena. Some felt that Dr. Chaney and Reverend Wallace had attuned themselves first to the audiences in either church, and when this was completed the messages were projected to them mentally by spirit beings hovering near them. Others felt that distance did not matter since a discarnate mind can project itself with lightning speed across the country and bring back the desired information.

Oliver Hasz told me that he had no explanation and expressed his amazement at the speed in which the messages came through. He had counted five different messages in ten minutes and speculated that the spirit beings had to be waiting in line to deliver their messages that rapidly.

I believe the most important point is that the projection of the human mind over this tremendous distance is possible and that apparently those physically dead are contacted as easily as those still in this life.

Dr. Chaney's and Reverend Wallace's attunement, which enabled them to describe "unknowable" details in distant churches, would seem to prove the unlimited reach of the human mind while it still inhabits the physical body.

THE SORCEROR'S MOON AND I

John O. Sangster

I sometimes have to pinch myself before I can believe that I am truly alive and well. My hair has whitened and my face is etched with the marks of suffering, but there was a time not so long ago when I would not have given a dime for my chances of surviving my ordeal by sorcery.

Even if I had not learned the fact from astrology, I could not have escaped the conclusion that my life is strongly influenced by the moon. I was born when the moon was full and my birth-date adds to the moon-number, two.

Most persons are aware of the strong influences that the moon exerts on fluids of all kinds. As a moon-subject my whole life has been strangely marked by the odd behavior of water, rain, bodily fluids, and other fluids. So much so, that I have suffered greatly from the fluids in my ears, nose, veins, and in the cavities of the head. Happily, all these troubles have cleared up since—but let me make a beginning.

I was barely a few weeks old when I commenced my travels over the seas that were to take me to every continent and to almost every corner of the globe. Water is the element specially ruled by the moon, and so it was that our satellite early commenced its rule over my life. Even as an ordinary cavalry trooper, I was transferred to no less than five countries during the First World War. During that war a shipwreck under the full moon, and a near-death by drowning on another occasion, were included in my program.

By some strange chance, although they were not chosen because of that fact, most of the many houses I lived in have had a stream or a river flowing at the bottom of the garden. It was not, however, until somewhat late in life that I realized the special connection that seems to exist between myself and water.

As a moon-subject of more than usual sensitivity, I found that I exert a strange influence over fluids, as though I am an instrument of the moon. I have never yet found a fountain pen that works properly for me—the flow of ink is either too little or too much; and when I open bottles of fizzy drinks, even though I hold them at an angle, the contents burst out before

I can do anything to stop them.

Whether I can go so far as to say that I have a certain local influence over weather, I do not know, but the fact remains that there have been many occasions when my movement from one place to another has coincided with a sudden and unexpected downpour of rain, though the sky had not been overcast beforehand. I also have had some success in dissolving clouds by concentrating my attention upon them.

Because of the moon-tempo that rules the rhythm of my body, my blood circulation is very slow in my arms and legs, and so I feel the rigors of winter keenly. Conversely, the heat of summer scarcely bothers me. True to my watery sign, I always succeed best when attempting to flow around difficulties rather than when trying to resolve them with frontal attacks.

I am a writer and all my best creative work is done after sundown. I never "sleep" at night in the sense of being totally unconscious, but I do not mind this and I feel every bit as refreshed in the mornings as though I had slept in the normal manner. In the evenings I am literally bursting with vitality and sparkling with joyous well-being.

Although I have lived a great deal in the tropics, the strong sun always gives me a curious sense of unease, and I cannot tolerate the seaside after the sun has gained its strength in the morning. I am also peculiarly sensitive to the setting sun, and there have been occasions when I have collapsed while having to look straight at the sun while it was on its way down to the horizon. I prefer gray, sunless days.

I am always plagued by nocturnal insects, birds and animals. Even the local inhabitants of my tropical homelands have been astonished to see a couple of dozen big frogs hopping over the floors of my house, and to see my walls and ceilings crawling with every kind of insect imaginable. Strange cats delight in coming through my windows so that they can sleep on my head or my belly, anywhere to be near me.

I am a marked man in more ways than one.

It is a curious thing, too, that I have been weather wise to an astonishing degree and this brings me to the point of my narrative—the recounting of those seven death-dealing years when I was the victim of diabolical sorcery.

The first indication that something unusual was happening to me was when I started having a peculiar and exceedingly painful feeling some six to twelve hours before it began to rain. In fact, I could predict the extent and intensity of the coming rain, or know that the overcast sky would clear up without any rain falling.

On those occasions, my head would feel as though it had been pumped full of water, and the feeling of pressure in my ears was more terrible than mere words can convey. It was frightening also because I could not seem to think or address myself to the simplest task.

Of course, I tried every means of diagnosis and treatment but no one could explain the trouble, and nothing could stay the dreaded daily summons to the torture chamber of relentless pain. You will better appreciate what this meant when I tell you that I was living in a country—Mauritius in the Indian Ocean—with an annual rainfall up to 180 inches.

Even the most powerful pain-killers were only partially effective, and in any case their daily use over a period of years is not to be thought of except as a method of suicide. When the attacks came on during the night I used to scream and groan with the dreadful pain and, in my utter helplessness, I felt as though I wanted to bang my head on the wall to bring unconsciousness. As the condition grew in intensity it affected my eyes, and the pain that I suffered in one or the other eyeball was the most agonizing of all, though perhaps not so terrifying as the frightful fluidic pressure and pain in my head.

As the years dragged by I tried my best to minimize my suffering by developing an attitude of detachment, but though this helped my morale, the pain was too intense to permit the mind to banish it with mental suggestions. The final stroke came when the area of pain spread to the occipital nerves at the back of my head. Ask any doctor to tell you the frightful nature of the pain these main sensory nerves can cause!

There were two things that sustained my spirit and prevented me from going insane during my years of agony: my firm belief in the goodness and love of God and the sweet love and courage of my wife. Something seemed to tell me that I must accept the severe spiritual test that I was being administered.

My physical state, however, was only one of my troubles. There was scarcely a single thing that did not go wrong in my affairs, and everything I did resulted in a loss of some kind. My wife watched aghast as a succession of calamities crushed nearly all my hopes in life. As though obeying some hidden power, nearly every circumstance of my daily activities led to frustration and negation. And yet I normally should have succeeded in so many of the things that I put my hand to, in spite of illness.

My wife and I kept a log of all those extraordinary happenings for which we could find no reasonable explanation and in one year we noted fifty-one such occurrences. In another period, nineteen important letters simply disappeared from the mails. Whatever plan I started, no matter how reasonable, simply came to naught. My state of black despair mounted, as

I saw myself and my life being reduced to zero.

But presently a pattern emerged from all these queer happenings. As you may well imagine, my wife and I were on the alert to find a proper moral and material cause, and we finally saw that something really extraordinary was going on. I came to realize that a powerful attempt was being made to break my spirit and to prevent me thinking creatively.

One day I chanced to meet a Hindu named Sukdeo Seegoolam who was engaged in healing work among the poor Indian laboring classes of Mauritius. I told him something about my troubles. He invited me to visit him daily at his little wooden hut, where there were never less than thirty to forty persons squatting on the ground waiting their turn to see him about their problems. He used to work right through from 9:00 a.m. to about 3:00 a.m. with a small break in the evening for his one meal of the day. In those early days I had no idea of the great powers of this wonderful man.

Seegoolam was a combination of saint, seer, psychologist, and spiritual healer. He used to heal his patients or solve their problems through prayer, the laying on of hands, and by communicating with discarnate entities while in trance. He invited me to help him in his work, for while he could effect cures in a few days, I had the unique gift of being able to eliminate almost all kinds of pain, in persons other than myself, within a few minutes. By such fast work I was able to earn him a long rest; and he then sat down to look more closely into my case.

The one room of his hut was arranged as a shrine, and the floor at one end served as an altar on which incense and candles were kept burning in brass holders. The walls were covered with colored prints of Christian saints, Hindu gods, and great yogis of India, and he seemed to extract power from each one of them for each particular purpose. There was no furniture, and one ate, slept, and sat on the floor.

At the end of my narrative, Seegoolam, a heavily-built man, went into a deep trance. Presently he commenced to speak and there was an expression of great sorrow in his voice and on his face. He shuddered and kept moving his head and his hands, as though appalled by what he saw and heard. His voice rose and fell with great gulps of emotion as he said, "Your spirit has a great destiny here on Earth but you have been held back by the hatred of a woman who scorns you with vitriolic rage because she could not bend you to her will. This woman consulted an evil Black Magician of great power and, for a large sum of money, he undertook to bind you in a straitjacket of suffering and misery. You were to be thrust into the blackest pit of hell, there to suffer loss, frustration, and the most miserable of lives. Your spirit was to be completely broken, your mind immobilized, and you were to be subjected to a slow, torturous death."

The voice of Seegoolam rose on a wailing, despairing note as he continued, "This woman gave that Black Magician your photograph, your birthdate, and certain details regarding your spheres of sensitivity and your ideals.

"The Magician, whose soul is bound in service to a group of malefic discarnate entities in the lower regions of the earth, then went into trance communication with the leader of this group to ask for his instructions.

"This leader, who had once wrought great evil on Earth, told the Black Magician to puncture the photograph at certain points of your head while the moon was invisible in your part of the earth, and to do so while uttering certain incantations. The fatalistic tarot number 18 was repeated during the incantations and each time that the photograph was pricked with a pin. (Tarot Number 18: *The image is a rayed moon from which drops of blood are falling; a wolf and a hungry dog are seen below catching the falling drops of blood in their opened mouths, while still lower a crab is seen hastening to join them. It is symbolic of materialism striving to destroy the spiritual side of the nature. It generally associates a person with bitter quarrels, and it is a sign of treachery, deception by others; also danger from the elements, such as storms, and water. —Cheiro*)

The head and hands of Seegoolam continued to sway with the force of his emotion and his voice then took on a low moaning tone, as he continued, "This woman was told by the Black Magician to concentrate her thoughts upon her desires concerning you. On a certain day, coinciding with the last quarter of the moon, she was to hang a board on which your name had been painted underneath a tree and to drive nails into each letter of your name while uttering the words of her curse.

"This had to be done at night during a torrential downpour, and while facing your part of the world. The board was then to be tied to a heavy stone and to be hurled at the reflection of the moon on the surface of a pond or stream."

Seegoolam's clothing was saturated with perspiration as he slowly came out of his trance. He passed his hand across his forehead and he looked at me with a quizzical expression, albeit with great tenderness, as he said, "Master, you are in very great trouble, but I can utterly destroy the power of this horrible curse if you are prepared to be very patient and to follow me faithfully and closely in all the things that I will require you to do.

"You will have to repose complete faith in me, even though most of my commands will appear strange to your Western mind and though they will put you to great inconvenience. The alternative to your acceptance would be the abandonment of all your hopes and dreams in this life and your premature end in a tragic death."

Seegoolam continued solemnly, "You know very well that your supersensitivity renders you too weak to fight your ordeal alone. I ask you, therefore, to choose wisely and well, and to renounce all fears as to the inevitability of your dreadful condition. You have helped me, dear Master, and you have taught me much. Now it is my turn to help you regain the happy creative life which is your birthright."

Of course, I hadn't the slightest hesitation, and you may imagine with what joy my wife and I agreed to place ourselves in his hands. As Seegoolam explained, the joining of our two souls in a harmonious and spiritual unity would be one of the strongest elements that he had to work with. There would be midnight masses for a month, ceremonies to be conducted at the edge of the sea at the setting of the sun, and I would have to undergo the whole procedure of spiritual cleansing seven times when the moon was at a certain phase. We both agreed to accept all conditions, to carry them out with faith and thankfulness to God.

As I came to know Seegoolam more intimately, I discovered that he was a White Magician treading the right-hand path of selfless devotion to God and humanity. All religions were the same to him and he looked for no reward or fame for himself.

There followed months during which I would kneel by his side while with his hands he became the instrument for the conveyance of spiritual force to me. Wonderful words of power were given to me, words that enhanced my faith in God and in myself. The healing balm of a great love flowed out from Seegoolam and, though as yet there was no sign of a cessation of my troubles, I had not the slightest doubt of my ultimate deliverance.

I shall never forget those memorable evenings on the beaches of Mauritius, when with Seegoolam on his knees, hands up-flung, with his eyes glowing in the ecstasy of sacred prayer, I attempted time and time again to sail my little bark of faith upon the dangerous waters of this world's tides; only to see it beaten back to the shore with its light extinguished. My little ship of hope, with which I was to test the timing of my deliverance, was made of a few green leaves of the betel tree pressed together. On these was placed a cube of burning camphor.

Then one evening, at long last, when the setting sun was a glory of fiery colors upon the far horizon I saw my little bark sail straight out to the

Lord of all Life, its light burning brightly and its course straight and true. Seegoolam gave a great shout and ran to embrace me. Only then did he allow his hands to fall and his prayers to cease.

From that moment onward I never suffered again.

Before Seegoolam left Mauritius, and so passed out of my life, he instructed me in some of the secrets of occultism and in the knowledge of what goes on in the invisible world that inter-penetrates our own world.

The occult powers and knowledge of Seegoolam were really far beyond the ordinary. He had the power to send his spirit to any part of the world and within a few minutes he could describe the interior details of a room thousands of miles away. He could describe and name the individuals and say what they were doing. On one occasion when in my presence he "visited" New York I was astonished to see his body slowly rise and fall on the floor in a gentle rhythmic motion. He afterwards told me that on crossing the Atlantic Ocean the wind had been so cold at high altitudes that he had been obliged to travel just above the waves. I had tried to press his body down to the floor but had been unable to do so.

Incidentally, it is only now that I can tell this true story because the person who caused me to become subject to the ordeal by sorcery passed out of this world as recently as December 17, 1959. I received the news with great pity because she died in terrible agony—from cancer.

All this has prompted me to think how precious we should hold the gift of life and with what great respect we should treat every hour as it passes.

GHOST SOLDIER IN OUR ATTIC

Etna Elliot

My husband and I, with our three children, left Portland, Ore., in the hot summer of 1928, to join my parents in the high mountains of California, five miles from Georgetown, where they had purchased a gold mine and were working it together with my uncle Charlie. There were no buildings at the mine and they rented an old farm which was badly in need of repairs. It had been unlived in for several years and my folks spent some time making it livable, so that it was real comfortable by the time we reached there with our family.

During the day, while the men were busy at the mine, Mother and I went to work in the attic, which we reached by a very narrow, steep stairway. We piled old trunks, boxes, a very tiny old-fashioned organ, an old music-box and other discarded articles of the departed family, all in one end of the attic.

As we were working, I suddenly felt as if someone had walked up behind me, but turning I saw nothing but the cobwebs which hung from the peak-roofed ceiling. I told Mother that I had the odd feeling of being watched, but she only looked at me queerly, then talked of other things.

Later on I ran downstairs to get something for Mother. As I came back up the steps someone brushed by me, almost knocking me back down the stairway. Still, I could not see a thing, although I had felt the contact distinctly.

We worked up in the attic for several days before we had it ready for use. During all that time, I felt an unseen presence near me. After what had happened on the stairway, I wouldn't let my Mother out of my sight and followed at her heels the whole time. We had put two beds side by side in the narrow room, leaving only a two-foot space between them. Then we hung thin lace curtains in the doorway to hide all the things piled in the other end of the attic. And still, air from the two windows at each end could circulate through the area where we were to sleep.

My husband did not like the idea of going up into that hot attic to sleep, so he put his bed under an old apple-tree near the front porch. Therefore, our small daughter and I slept in one bed and our two boys in the other. That first night I was terribly nervous, so Mother turned the kerosene lamp down low and said, "Just leave it burn if you will feel better." But even with the light burning I still could feel that unseen presence and I don't think I slept over five minutes that whole night. I was terribly tired the next day; still I could hardly bring myself to go to bed that next night.

Finally the children could not be kept up any longer and I slowly climbed those steep stairs, with cold chills running up into my hair. I got the children into bed and climbed in beside my little daughter. I forced myself to close my eyes and finally fell asleep, only to be awakened much later by an icy wind blowing over my body.

With my eyes wide open, in the dim light of the kerosene lamp, I saw him!

Standing just outside the lace curtains was a young soldier in uniform. He was tall and straight and looking intently at me as if he were about to speak. The curtains blew out toward me and he started moving in my direction. I screamed and then was unable to move until my parents came dashing up the stairs. I sobbed out what I had seen and I thought there was a look of horror on their faces. My mother slept up in the attic with us the rest of the night, but she wouldn't talk much about it the next day.

The following night I forced my feet up the stairs. I did not want the children to know how frightened I was. Mother stayed up there with us until the children were asleep and I had become quite calm. I tried to make myself believe that I had imagined the whole thing, and when morning came and there had been no frightening experiences during the night I almost believed this.

A week passed. I was feeling quite safe as we went to bed, and almost at once I fell into a sound sleep, only to be awakened about two o'clock in the morning.

I felt as if someone had shaken me. I sat right up in bed, wide awake and trembling. My body was as cold as ice.

There, sitting on the edge of the other bed, right against my small son, was the same young soldier. He was looking into my face, smiling, and he had his elbow on his knee. He held a hat in his hand, which he was swinging back and forth. I recognized the hat as a soldier's hat of World War I. It had a wide brim with a heavy, bright cord around the crown. It, or a hat like it, had been hanging in the hall when my parents moved into the house and I had been wearing it as a sun hat since coming to the mines.

Now this ghostly soldier had the same hat in his hand as he smiled at me, his face not over a foot from my own. He leaned toward me, closer and closer!

I have never remembered making a sound but I must have for my parents were soon there. This time I could see the soldier long after they were in the room.

I was weak and trembling for several days after that and my dad put up a cot at the other end of the attic, just outside the lace curtains, and slept there himself every night. So things settled down and I was beginning to think and hope I would not see the soldier again.

When I quietly slipped into bed beside my little daughter on this particular night I felt safe with my dad so near. Turning on my side with my face to the wall, I was soon fast asleep. But sometime in the early morning hours I was suddenly wide awake and again as cold as ice. A large, heavy hand was pressing down on my shoulder. I tried to rise but I was held tight by this pressure. Turning my face up, I found myself looking right into the eyes of the soldier. His face was only inches from mine and I still felt his hand as plainly as I have ever felt the hand of my husband. I felt as if I were dying.

I still think I would have died, and that the soldier would have taken me with him, except that at that very instant my small daughter sat up in bed screaming the most unearthly screams I have ever heard. Still it seemed her screams receded farther and farther from me.

To this day, that child, now a grown woman, thinks a soldier was taking me away.

Her screams, of course, brought Dad and Mother, and my mother had her arms around me before that soldier took his hand from my shoulder.

They finally got me downstairs and in my hysterical condition I managed to make them understand that I wanted the children brought down at once. My dad and husband hurried to do this, and my mother held my little daughter until she cried herself to sleep. We all sat in the kitchen the rest of that awful night.

My husband was very doubtful of what I had seen. He said that he wanted to sleep upstairs the next night and see for himself what was going on. I begged him not to, but he was determined. He went off to bed and the next morning said he had slept fine. This continued for almost a week. Then one night about midnight he came bounding down the stairs, blankets and all. We never could get him to say what he had seen or what had happened. He was very pale and said only that he would never sleep up there again, that this so-and-so house should be burned and the ashes buried.

Then in the bright light of day my parents told us what the old lady had said to them when they rented the house. She had looked at them for a long time and then said, "You are welcome to live in the place if you can stand it!"

Pointing to great piles of rocks all over the place, she continued, "See those rocks? Well, I have piled them just to have something to do, to keep me out of the house. For my husband still lives there, although he has been dead many years." Then she added, "Yes, and the boys come back too, so I have left the house to them most of the time."

She explained that her husband had died in a drunken stupor in that house; one of her sons had dropped dead on the back porch; her youngest son had died in the kitchen while having a fist fight with his brother; and her oldest son, a soldier in World War I, had come home after being wounded and died in his sleep in his bed in the attic.

"This house is bad!" she had gone on to say. "But if you can stand to live among them, you are welcome." Now at last my parents believed her. The men went to work at once and built a large cabin at the mine. My husband and I stayed there only long enough to help my parents move out of that house with its ghostly inhabitants before returning gratefully to our home in Portland.

CANADA'S UNKNOWN STIGMATIST

Alex Saunders

Recently the editors of FATE were informed that a Canadian farm woman living in Uptergrove, near Toronto, Ontario, has displayed, in comparative secrecy, for almost two decades, stigmatic phenomena that reportedly are as remarkable as those of the famed stigmatist Therese Neumann of Konnersreuth, Germany.

In an effort to obtain an up-to-date story on the Canadian stigmatist, FATE'S editors in June, 1958, assigned Toronto writer Alex Saunders to investigate. His report follows:

"Some eighty-odd miles north of Toronto, between Lakes Simcoe and Couchiching, lies the village of Uptergrove. Unknown to most people is the fact that this quiet community of approximately three hundred is distinguished by having as a resident one of the world's few living stigmatists, a Mrs. Donald McIsaac. North America, it appears, can boast of no other.

"I phoned Mrs. McIsaac long-distance for an interview. She made it clear that she was uninterested and wanted no publicity.

"Despite this, I visited Uptergrove on Saturday, June 21, and, having been given directions, went directly to the farm on which she lives.

"A knock at the door brought out one of her sons, a friendly, pleasant-looking fellow who appeared to be in his late twenties. I explained the reason for my presence.

"He admitted that his Roman Catholic mother was a stigmatist and that the phenomena still occur at the present time. His voice became more firm when he said that what the McIsaac family wanted most was to be left alone. In short—no publicity.

"Mrs. McIsaac was through with granting interviews. Although the woman presently was in the house, her son thought it best that she should not meet me, as he did not wish to have her upset.

"I gave my solemn word to write the facts as they really were and to mail Mrs. McIsaac the final script for her approval. Only then, with her written permission, would I send the article to FATE. This offer was rejected.

"Taking a photo of the farmhouse was also politely forbidden. The son was very firm and stubbornly refused to hear more. He went indoors.

"My next stop was the Adams General Store & Post Office where I spoke to the proprietors, Mr. and Mrs. Adams. Like most villagers, they were warm and hospitable. I was given some additional information, but nothing of actual substance.

"I was assured that the entire small community was aware that a stigmatist lived among them, but had kept silent in respect for her feelings.

"It appears that other articles published some years ago created quite a fuss. A steady flow of the curious caused much disturbance in the village. The McIsaac family was so plagued with phone calls that they were forced to have their number changed.

"Friends deserted Mrs. McIsaac; relatives took sides. There was much bigotry. Mrs. McIsaac felt compelled to leave her church and join a more distant one.

"My suggestion that I visit her former church in order to talk to the priest was discouraged. I was told he had died a few years before and had been replaced.

"My questioning of a few other villagers brought nothing new to light. Answers were given reluctantly. It was obvious that Uptergrove residents desired no recurrence of the furor stirred up previously."

Mrs. McIsaac, apparently, is fully stigmatized, as is Therese Neumann. Those who have seen the wounds of both describe them as being very similar.

Stigmata are associated with the wounds suffered by Christ during His crucifixion. They represent the injuries caused by the crown of thorns, the scourging at the pillar, the nails of the cross and the spear thrust into Christ's side. Thus, when stigmatization is complete, the wounds are present in some seven different parts of the body.

Some stigmatists may have wounds in as many as five places, some in as few as one.

In addition, Mrs. McIsaac is said to bear a wound which appears only on Good Friday and vanishes by Easter. This wound, a large one which bleeds, is on the right shoulder, the shoulder upon which Christ carried the Cross.

Numerous doctors and churchmen have studied Mrs. McIsaac's wounds. Few believe they have a supernatural origin, but the outright skeptics as yet have failed to give a conclusive and generally acceptable medical explanation.

Mrs. Donald McIsaac is 57 years old and is described as short and stout. Her paternal grandfather was a full-blooded Huron Indian. Her husband is a farmer and they have six living children. She attended only the Canadian equivalent of grammar school, where she was considered an average student. She is said to be a cheerful and busy housewife despite the almost twenty years of suffering caused by her wounds.

Apparently, Mrs. McIsaac's stigmata first appeared in 1937. She had a religious vision and a short time later a painful sore appeared on her right hand. She visited several doctors, who prescribed various medications and treatments, but the sore refused to heal.

Within the next three years other stigmata appeared. The wounds deepened until her hands and feet were pierced through. She was unable to grasp objects tightly and walking was difficult. Bleeding when touched, the wounds were painful, particularly the one in her side. The last of Mrs. McIsaac's stigmata are said to have appeared in 1940. By this time the pain and bleeding had diminished, appearing only weekly on Fridays between 6:00 and 9:00 p.m., and yearly from 11:00 p.m. on Holy Thursday to 12:00 midnight on Good Friday. For six days a week Mrs. McIsaac is said to be much like any ordinary farm housewife. Her wounds are visible but they do not bleed and she feels no pain.

Rev. M. J. Nealon, then parish priest of Uptergrove, took an interest in Mrs. McIsaac's stigmata from the beginning. By 1940 he was convinced that they were genuine and he called them to the attention of his superiors. Although the Roman Catholic Church takes no official notice of such phenomena, it does investigate them quietly and carefully in an effort to unmask fakes. In the past thirty years some fifty fraudulent stigmatists have been exposed by the Church.

In 1943 Cardinal McGuigan of the Archdiocese of Toronto became interested in the claims concerning Mrs. McIsaac and arranged to investigate them. She was given intensive examinations at St. Michael's Hospital in Toronto and at Bresica Hall, a Catholic women's college. Doctors on the boards of these institutions gave the Church signed statements describing what they had witnessed.

During three weeks of observation in 1945 and two in 1946, Mrs. McIsaac was watched closely every minute day and night. The examining doctors—who were of Catholic, Protestant and Jewish faiths—made a wide variety of tests. In one test blood smears taken during the Friday agonies were compared with smears taken on other days. In another test the time at which the agonies began and ended—always 6:00 and 9:00 p.m.—was studied. Mrs. McIsaac was not allowed to have a clock or a watch in her room and the daily schedule of her meals and other matters was changed in an effort to mislead her into thinking it was later in the day than it actually was.

Nevertheless her agonies began and at 6:00 and ended at 9:00 p.m. exactly.

One of the investigating medical specialists, a Protestant, described Mrs. McIsaac's wounds as peculiar. The wounds on the backs of her hands, he said, were square, dark and somewhat hard, while those on the palms were smaller, of a reddish color and covered with a transparent tissue. This was true also of the wounds on Mrs. McIsaac's insteps and soles.

The wound in her left side, according to the specialist, was deep, long, and narrow. Around her head, at the hairline, were many small, circular wounds. On her back were several crisscrossing wounds suggestive of lash marks.

Another Protestant doctor reported that through the course of a week, up to late Friday afternoon, Mrs. McIsaac was in excellent health despite her wounds. She was found to be completely normal, except for being somewhat deaf and having weak eyes. Alert and energetic, she spoke readily and cheerfully. Her conversation indicated she was devoutly religious.

On Friday afternoon, the doctor's report continued, a change was noticed in the marks on Mrs. McIsaac's body. They began to soften and as 6:00 p.m. approached they began to look fresh. Mrs. McIsaac's expression and movements now indicated that she was beginning to feel pain. The pain increased and became agony. She fell into what appeared to be a trance. Tiny drops of blood appeared at the wounds on her hairline and on her feet. Then the wounds on her hands and elsewhere on her body began to bleed.

Mrs. McIsaac's wounds, the doctor observed, bled copiously, except those on her back which oozed only a few drops. By 9:00 p.m. blood from her head wounds covered Mrs. McIsaac's face and matted her hair.

At intervals during the period from 6:00 to 9:00 p.m. Mrs. McIsaac sat up in bed and stretched out her arms as if reaching toward something in front of her. While in her trance she did not reply to questions, and was unaware of noises or of being touched. Although her eyes were open, she did not blink when a hand or a lighted match was passed in front of them.

Occasionally Mrs. McIsaac regained consciousness, her pain evidently having diminished. She answered questions and described what she had seen during her trance. Each of these lucid moments was followed by increased agony and bleeding until finally she became completely unconscious.

Around 9:00 p.m. the bleeding lessened and finally stopped. Mrs. McIsaac's pain also appeared to lessen and she fell into a normal sleep. Not long afterward she woke and, questioned about the lucid intervals between the trance states, said that she remembered everything she had said. She described her visions in greater detail. She seemed exhausted and that night she slept soundly. On Saturday morning, the doctor said, he was surprised to find her looking fresh and rejuvenated. An examination showed she was in excellent health.

The doctors who investigated Mrs. McIsaac expressed belief that her wounds were not supernatural in nature. However, they also were certain there was no possibility of deception. As one of them pointed out, Mrs. McIsaac was observed constantly by trained and experienced persons. Her bleeding was studied at close range, and microscopic examination proved that there had been an actual flow of blood. If the bleeding had been artificially produced, it would have left a different type of scar. There also would have been some infection, no trace of which was found. Moreover, the wounds healed more quickly than would have been the case in wounds artificially caused.

The specialists had no certain or final explanation for the phenomena they observed in Mrs. McIsaac. They stated they knew of no disease which would account for such wounds or their periodic bleeding. Stigmata cases, one pointed out, are rare and have not been subjected to large-scale, organized study.

Some doctors, noting that the greater majority of stigmatists are women, incline to the belief that the phenomena may be associated with the physiological process in women called the "change of life." This, however, does not explain the existence of the phenomena in men also. Other doctors explain stigmatization on the basis of such psychological processes as autosuggestion, hallucination, self-hypnosis, hysteria, and martyr-complex. These doctors believe that, in the case of stigmatists, the subconscious mind influences the higher nerve centers controlling nutrition in certain parts of the body in such a way as to cause wounds and periodic bleeding. Another explanation is that stigmatization may be the result of such rare skin disorders as autographism and dermographism, which are the result of religious hysteria.

Women hysterics as a rule display such abnormal symptoms as restlessness, suspicion, anxiety and emotional instability. However, both psychiatrists and doctors report having found Mrs. McIsaac to be mentally normal. She would have to be hopelessly abnormal, they said, to produce stigmatization phenomena fraudulently.

Roman Catholic Church authorities also differ in their opinions regarding stigmatization phenomena such as that displayed by Mrs. McIsaac. Some priests feel there is a natural explanation while others believe the wounds have a supernatural basis. The Church itself does not confirm or deny that stigmata may be supernatural in origin. Neither does it overlook the possibility that such phenomena may be due to natural causes.

A standard policy of the Church is not to grant official recognition to saints, miracle-workers, or stigmatists during their lifetimes. Therese Neumann, although honored by the highest dignitaries of the Church, has never been officially recognized.

Although the Church investigates cases like that of Mrs. McIsaac during the lifetime of the subjects, it releases no pronouncements until many years after their deaths. In the cases of those accepted as true stigmatists, the Church rules out a natural explanation. Many of the stigmatists honored by the Church received their wounds after a sickness or injury, while others received them in normal health.

Many Church authorities believe that stigmata are bestowed upon highly devout persons not so much because of their great love for Christ as for the sake of the many who will be inspired by the message. For this reason the Church regards the mystical or ecstatic side of the phenomena as equal in importance to the physical side. The Church believes that all true stigmatists experience ecstasies or visions and receive their stigmata while undergoing such an experience.

A priest who investigated the mystical side of Mrs. McIsaac's stigmatic manifestations reported that he was convinced that she became an ecstatic when she received her first wounds. Mrs. McIsaac, he said, displayed three states which usually are associated with stigmatization in the mystical sense. In the first of these states, "complete ecstasy"—reached on Fridays when her wounds bleed—her agonies are accompanied by visions of the Passion of Christ and other scenes from Church history. The state begins with the mystical condition called the *raptus,* "an instantaneous surrender of the whole being to a supernatural compulsion." It comes over her suddenly, often in the middle of a sentence. While in this state she is unaware of being questioned or touched.

The second state, "prepossession," was found to occur mostly during breaks in the Friday agonies and immediately afterward. Mrs. McIsaac speaks and is aware but displays a lack of the knowledge that is acquired through experience. She answers questions about her visions with a childlike simplicity. The contents of the visions conform to the liturgical season in which they occur and are said to be accurate in details of architecture, dress, and language. Mrs. McIsaac has claimed to hear the Aramaic vernacular spoken at the time of Christ, and to be able to distinguish dialects of the tongue.

The third state is described as "exalted rest," an ecstatic sleep or coma. This often occurs after Mrs. McIsaac has received Holy Communion. Although her eyes are closed, she talks and gestures animatedly, often exhibiting an extrasensory awareness of persons and events.

In his book, *La Stigmatisation,* published in 1894, Dr. A. Imbert-Gourbeyre, of Paris, stated that since the stigmatization of St. Francis of Assisi in 1224 there had been 321 authentic stigmatists, 41 of whom were men. St. Francis of Assisi is considered the first stigmatist, but St. Paul claimed in a letter to the Galatians that his body bore the marks of Jesus' crucifixion.

Some of the most famed stigmatists of the 19th century were Anna Catherine Emmerich of Germany, Sister Maria Fidelis Weiss of Bavaria, Louise Lateau of Belgium and Maria von Moerl of Switzerland. Two internationally renowned stigmatists of today are Therese Neumann, who has borne the marks since March, 1926, and the Capuchin Monk, Padre Pio of Foggia, Italy, who has had them since 1918. There may be other modem stigmatists as yet unknown to the world.

The Catholic Church prefers that stigmatists remain in obscurity. From the first it made every effort to shield Mrs. McIsaac from public notice. However, news of the miraculous phenomena surrounding her has spread by means of a sort of religious grapevine. In the past two decades she has been visited by many thousands from all parts of the world. The pilgrims have ranged from high churchmen to priests and nuns, from medical specialists to persons seeking miracle cures. Although the Church disapproves of such visits it has not banned them.

In recent years, only persons officially connected with the Church have been permitted to see Mrs. McIsaac. Even these must prove their identity. Few lay persons are admitted to her home, only those whose interest is purely religious.

Mrs. McIsaac gives no interviews to members of the press. She and her family feel that reporters have twisted and exaggerated the facts in connection with her stigmatic phenomena. Articles which have been published about Mrs. McIsaac have caused much disturbance and neither she nor her family wishes a recurrence of this. Even the townsfolk, weary of constant questions and interruptions of their quiet routine, have grown reticent.

Such are the available details about one of the few persons in the world today considered to be an authentic stigmatic.

I OWE MY LIFE TO A DOG

J. P. J. Chapman

Most people, at some time or other, have had such narrow escapes from death that seconds were of vital importance. Personally I have had quite a few narrow squeaks; my most memorable escape I owe to a dog.

It happened in late October, 1918. I was a mechanic in an air squadron. The Germans were in heavy retreat. I was sent, with some other men, to an advance emergency landing ground behind Cambrai. There were perhaps twenty-five of us in all. Extra hands in the cook house worked on a rotation basis. Eventually, of course, my turn came.

The cook house was nothing more than a knock-up tin shanty, one end open, where one got boiled on one side and frozen on the other.

The squadron had picked up a hungry mongrel some months before. He was such a lovable dog that he was unofficially "put on the strength." Naturally, he knew what was good for him and spent most of his time in the cook house—unless he was fighting with some interloper who wanted to muscle in.

Snuffer, as he was soon named because of his favorite activity, selected a few personal friends. I was honored to be one of these.

The emergency landing ground was rather a hot spot, in full view of German Observation "Sausages" five miles in front of us. But, perhaps as no effort had been made to put up a "show," Jerry left us alone.

On my day in the cook house as general factotum, helping the so-called cook, Jerry had a long range gun about two miles on the other side of the German lines. It was our job to spot and if possible put it out of action. This gun was not fired at any particular target but shells were lobbed over at various points in the hope of a "hit."

At about 11 a.m. a couple of shells burst a quarter of a mile away.

"Cor! Blimey!" remarked our cockney cook. "Gettin' a bit 'ot, ain't it, mate?"

I said there was consolation in the fact that the one that had our number on it we would never hear!

Shortly after this our dog became restless, walking around the boilers, in and out of the shed, and generally acting fussy. Finally he sat down and started to howl like a forlorn wolf.

"Well, strike me pink! Wot's the matter with the dawg ter day?" asked cook.

"Seems to me," I replied, "he knows something we don't."

After about five minutes of steady howling the dog got up and went over to cook and turned around and around his legs. A few moments later Snuffer came over to me and started barking furiously. I bent down to stroke him, wondering what it was all about. No sooner did I put out my hand than the dog took it in his mouth—very gently—and gave every indication that I should come away with him.

I looked at cook and said, "Here, come on, Bill. He's got a line somewhere. Let's follow. The grub won't be any more spoilt for a while."

The dog let go of my hand and we followed him to a shellhole about twenty-five yards from the cook house.

In we went. After we were there some few minutes Bill thought he would go. The dog immediately became quite fierce, showed his teeth and growled. Bill sat back down. Snuffer subsided.

It was not too bad in the hole, protected from the nasty wind. We had some fags, and so we smoked away the time.

But after a few minutes more Snuffer looked up at the sky, then looked at me. Immediately we heard a whine and then a terrible crash. A shell had hit the cook house right plumb in the middle. Bill and I sat just looking at each other. After this event the dog took no further interest in us. He got up and rushed to the wreckage of the demolished cook house to forage what he could find. It was doubtless the biggest "blowout" he had had for many a day.

Sometime later, after we entered Germany, I became a hospital case. Before going, I went to Snuffer and told him it was goodbye. I think he understood. He licked my hand and sat back on his haunches and let off the most dismal howl I have ever heard.

Well, that was more than forty years ago, but I can still see every bit of it, every plank and sheet of iron, just as if it had been yesterday. Snuffer was a wonderful dog and one of nature's gentlemen. If ever a dog deserved a "Doggy Heaven," with a super cook house, he did. I hope he has one!

MAGIC AND PRAYER IN THE LAND OF MAYAS

Mary L. Gebow

Curiosity started the strangest and most puzzling experience of my life. I had heard about the founding of a new and different kind of university in San Francisco, intended for adults only. A university which did not offer degrees—only a broad education in science, psychology, sociology, law, and history, with a special emphasis in parapsychology. It was founded by a businessman from San Francisco, and, what was even more interesting, it was reported that the university did not pay its professors. I was curious and went to hear a lecture by the university's founder and Chairman of the Department of World Religions, Dr. Eugene E. Whitworth.

What did I expect? I do not know, but I was not prepared for a six-foot, dynamic and direct man in a blue business suit, who spoke in simple sentences and told an amazing story.

Great Western University was founded by businessmen and educators in San Francisco, men of every church and faith who pooled their efforts to make available a good university-level education at very low cost. No one who worked for the university was paid for his efforts, yet many brilliant men from all over the United States had joined in the hard work of writing, editing, and organizing its courses.

Dr. Whitworth said, "Great Western University does not offer degrees, it offers a new approach to everyday life." Then, quite casually, he spoke about a projected trip into the hazardous Lacandone forest to do research on the dying religion of the ancient Mayas.

The Lacandones are a remnant of the once powerful Mayan nation. They are far removed from civilization, in a very dangerous part of the State of Chiapas, in lower Mexico. The Lacandones still practice some of the ancient rituals. The purpose of the expedition was to photograph these rituals. I'm a professional photographer and I love to travel, but such a trip was far from my mind.

But as Dr. Whitworth outlined the trip, I suddenly knew I just had to go. Crazy? Certainly! I would have to quit my job as engineering draftsman in Richmond, Calif. But I had to go. So after the lecture I went up to Dr. Whitworth and asked if there was a place for me on the expedition.

"You'd have to pay your own way. And it's quite hazardous," he warned.

"I know. The books call it the Green Hell," I said. "Can I go?"

For a long time he stood looking at me. Not just at, but through and beyond me. He turned to his wife and they spoke quietly for a few seconds. Then both stood as if in the attitude of prayer. After a moment he said quietly, "If you wish you may go."

That was my introduction to the God-filled Whitworths. They are now my beloved and laughter-filled Ruth and Gene. We've been through that Green Hell together. It was dangerous, deadly and thrilling. But to me the most thrilling thing in my whole life—and also the most puzzling—is: How can there be such a strange mixture of God in man? But I am ahead of my story.

When I told my boss and my friends that I was going with an expedition from Great Western University into the Lacandone jungle they simply flipped. They thought I'd gone mad, and said so. Some said, "Now, now, Mary, think it over." Others said frankly, "You've a game leg." (I had a bout with polio and my left leg gives out easily.) Still others spoke of "all those snakes, spiders and scorpions." "If you go on that crazy expedition, you're plain nuts!" they said. They tried to convince me that only a crackpot would quit a job to undertake a dangerous mission just to study the religion of a dying race.

I set out to find all the information I could about Dr. and Mrs. Eugene E. Whitworth. It wasn't hard. Ruth Whitworth was born in Toledo, Oh. She came west as a Wave and finally took a degree in art from the California College of Arts and Crafts. Dr. Whitworth came from Texas and had lived in the Bay Area since 1926. He attended and holds degrees from the University of California, Stanford University, and Lincoln University. Furthermore, he was well known to many people in Richmond, Calif., where I worked. For twenty years he had held a very responsible job in a large company in San Francisco. The more I found out about them the more solid and substantial they seemed. I decided that I'd go on the expedition despite my friends' advice.

Nevertheless, after I had quit my job and on the day the expedition was to leave San Francisco, February 2, 1959, I had a big lump of lead where my heart should have been.

To add to my fears, on the fourth day of the trip I lost my purse and all the money I had in the world. I thought I'd have to go home. We all knew that we were to pay our share. Great Western University does not pay anybody, and I now had no money to pay my expenses. But the Whitworths turned the whole tragic affair into a joke. They began to pay my share from their own pockets without a grumble or a word of reprimand for my carelessness. They did even more. Before the expedition had been travelling for long, they arranged for me to be paid by people who joined the expedition for a short while and rode in my car. Soon I had money in my pocket, courage in my heart, and a great admiration for two people who exhibited such indifference to money.

My admiration grew daily—and with it my puzzlement. And, at the same time, I had to call up courage I never knew I had. The Lacandone jungle can be a deadly place. It is possible to get lost only fifty yards from a good trail. So we who were on the expedition had to learn to live on our own, and from the jungle itself. The Whitworths put the members of the expedition through some of the toughest training courses for survival I've ever heard of. But it was done with so much laughter, so much God-consciousness, that no one on the expedition really minded the rugged hardening we had. We camped on the Rio Grijalva, below Tuxtla Gutierrez, and tried to get accustomed to the gengenes. They make little holes in the skin and lay eggs there. The welts itch something awful and may swell up like boils. Then we ran into the land of the Zinacantans. Near the place where we had our camp, some two years before, a white man had been beheaded by the natives. Here our purpose was dual. First, we had to learn to live with danger and hardship. Second, more complicated and important, the Whitworths wanted us to have a chance to learn to *feel* what the natives were thinking.

Under Dr. Whitworth's direction, Great Western University carries on a great amount of research in extrasensory perception. They make careful and scientific studies of the sending and receiving of thought-force messages. We were going into the Lacandone area where thought-force was part of the religion and daily life.

In the case of the Zinacantans, the thinking wasn't nice. They wanted us to pay $4.00 for each picture we took. We didn't—we couldn't—and we took from them only very good experience in understanding native behavior.

When the Whitworths thought we were tough enough for the jungle and could feel our way with the natives, more or less through thought-force contact, the Big Day was set for the real push, as the members of the expedition called it. We started into the Lacandone rainforest.

Our purpose was to photograph sacred religious rituals. It is hard to get permission to do this in any tribe. No one likes to have his holy rituals photographed by strangers. To meet this problem, the Whitworths had contacted many people in Mexico and Guatemala, trying to locate the person who could help them the most. Also, they wanted to be certain of getting only the true and authentic rituals. By letter they had located and agreed to meet in the jungle a Mr. Robert Bruce, of Sapulpa, Okla.

We stopped in San Cristobal de Las Casas to find out what Dr. and Mrs. Frans Blom—two of the great authorities on the Lacandones—knew of our possible guide. Robert Bruce had lived with the Lacandones almost constantly for five years. He lived as a native, wore their cotton gown, let his hair grow long, and went barefoot, so that he would be accepted by the Lacandones. He helped the natives in many ways, administering medicines and helping ease their burden of work. His friendship with the Lacandones seemed to be our best hope of getting the Sacred Ceremonies we wanted to make into motion pictures. However, we also found that he could not come out of the jungle to meet the expedition because he was wanted by the law in the State of Chiapas. We were to meet him somewhere in the jungle.

Dr. and Mrs. Whitworth prayed over this situation and then decided we would go on in. Later we were to discover that even after we got to the jungle we still had to arrange a special method of meeting. We were to send into the jungle a bottle of medicinal brandy, signed by Dr. Whitworth. Only then would Robert Bruce come out to meet us.

But as our expedition, which never numbered more than nine persons, neared the jungle, Dr. Whitworth said, "Bruce will come out to meet us. He'll meet us twenty-five miles from the place we are to go."

And he did! It made my eyes pop. One afternoon Robert Bruce came to the ranch where we were staying. He had walked twenty-five miles since early morning.

"I just had to come. I felt pushed," he said.

The expedition flew in light planes to the Lake Naja region. Because Lake Naja is equipped with running water, the women of the expedition were able to set up a bath and laundry room. Lake Naja has alligators. It also has a two-inch insect which the Lacandones fear more than they fear the coral snake, viper, or deadly fer-de-lance. They say its bite is sure death and that there is no antidote. This bug, they said, comes out of the lake only at night and in the rain. This was small cheer because a rain-filled storm called a *norte* was over us most of the time! The Lacandone name for this deadly insect was *mokelchiha*.

And there was always the danger of snakes. Three weeks before we got there a native woman had died from the bite of a fer-de-lance. The snake had been beside the trail we now took to go to the spring for our drinking water. We were all a little nervous but the Whitworths laughed and said, "No need to worry. We're being lovingly protected. You won't see anything."

They didn't explain. But it was as if that entire jungle had been swept clean. Not one of the members of our expedition ever saw a spider, a scorpion, or a snake! We lived right with the natives. They told of seeing snakes; a dog was bitten, a native cut a snake in two with his machete. But we of the expedition lived, ate, slept and worked with the Lacandones for eleven days—and we couldn't find snakes even when we looked!

When the expedition came to Naja we should have been ready for anything. We'd seen the future accurately pre-told on several occasions. But Dr. Whitworth still gave us a great scare on the day of our arrival. We'd brought up a load of equipment, backpacking it over the six hundred yards of four-inch round poles laid over the quicksand that surrounds Lake Naja. Gene came up last from the *cayucos* (log canoes). He was carrying a heavy back pack and two bags of camera equipment. We saw him going toward the *champa* (house) in the *caribal* (village) where we were to live with a Lacandone family. But when we returned from the second trip over that quicksand to get supplies from the *cayucos* he was gone.

We started our fire. As time went on and night approached, we all began to worry. All, that is, except his wife. Ruth said, "He's all right. Otherwise I'd know!" But we remained pretty upset. About two hours later Dr. Whitworth came into the *champa* and asked for a handful of vitamins and minerals from the expedition's supply. When we asked "what's up?" he said with a wry grin, "Oh, just a little witchcraft."

We found out later that he was fighting a thought-force battle for the right to film the sacred ceremonies of the Lacandones.

A young *kika* (woman) had lost her baby, on two different occasions, on the very first day of her third month. It was now just two days before the first day of her third month and she was about to lose her third child. She was terribly sick, suffering from awful cramps, and she was very much afraid. She and all the Lacandones thought and said that she had been bewitched and would surely lose her third child.

Robert Bruce was in the *champa* with Dr. Whitworth at the time the healing began. Later he told us, "I knew that unless he was able to help that woman and save the baby the Lacandones would never allow him to take motion pictures of their sacred ceremonies. It was a tough spot for any person to be put in."

Dr. Whitworth carefully questioned the *kika* and her *kiko* (man). It was a fairly difficult procedure. Robert Bruce acted as translator. To be certain that all questions were clearly answered, they also were put to the *kiko* in

Spanish, which Dr. Whitworth speaks fairly well. When he was certain that he had the whole story, Dr. Whitworth told the frightened woman to lie on the board the Lacandones use for a bed. He knelt beside her and seemed to pray. Then he began to massage her abdomen gently.

"The instant he touched her," Bruce said later, "the pain seemed to go— instantly, just like that! The *kika* knew it. You should have seen the look of joy and relief on her face. She knew something wonderful was taking place and her eyes lit up. After a while Dr. Whitworth had me tell her over and over in her own Mayan tongue that she would not lose her child; that no witchcraft could possibly work against the holy and perfect magic his God had put into his hands. He had me tell her over and over again that his God and her Supreme High God were the same, but with a different name. Over and over we told her this in Mayan. Then we had her *kiko* tell her the same things by explaining it to him in Spanish. It sounded like hypnosis, pure and simple. But it worked like true magic! In a very few minutes I could sense that the woman was all right. But he gave her massive doses of vitamins and minerals. Two hours later we left her dozing and relaxed."

When Dr. Whitworth and Robert Bruce came down to dinner we got this story. We all knew that the films—the success, the very purpose of the expedition—depended upon how effective was the magic of Dr. Whitworth's hands. After travelling almost five thousand miles possibly we all had a right to worry. As the two days crawled slowly by, only Ruth and Gene seemed calm.

"God gave him healing," Ruth said to me quietly. "He really has magic!"

The first day of the third month of the woman's pregnancy dawned hot and moist. We spent the time readying our camera equipment until the sun finally touched the rim of the mountains. In the setting sunlight we saw the *kika* walking slowly toward the spring for a jug of water. We knew the magic was good so far. And that very night every Lacandone in the *caribal* was around our campfire—with the sole exception of the *kika* herself. She was resting, as Dr. Whitworth had told her to do. We could see that the Lacandones were awed by his powers. They paid him every respect.

"They admire the God-given power, that's all. We all have the skill I used. We just don't use it with expectation." That's all the explanation Dr. Whitworth gave. He turned immediately to other things. But I thought it over many a night as I lay in my sleeping bag and the stars seemed to hang in the tree tops and God seemed all around.

That night the Lacandones talked to Dr. Whitworth for several hours about their own religion. He soon was explaining to them some of the symbols and meanings of their religious practices. They were awe-struck. We were all amazed at what he knew. Mr. Vicente Doria, of Bayonne, N.J., our special guide, had studied the Lacandone religion for four years. Robert Bruce had lived with them for five years. Both were incredulous. "How could you learn so much about these rituals and symbols?" they demanded. "This has never been written down that we know of, and you've never seen it before...?"

Gene merely shrugged. "God has the answers."

They both said that they had never seen any man so much loved as Gene was by those wonderful, gentle Lacandones. Where he walked they turned their faces in respect. He seemed to them to be one of their own saints in the flesh. They decided to open to him their sacred ceremony to be photographed. That very night they agreed to perform, for the expedition cameras, the famous *Cuxuh* (God Hat) ceremony.

The preparations and ceremony take four days. They began the next morning. The *Cuxuh* must be performed under the God Hut—the temple of the Lacandones. It begins with the gathering of four things from the forest.

First they cut sugar cane from the sacred groves. It is peeled and placed in the God Hut, in front of the God Pots, to remain overnight so the spirit of the Most High God may enter into it.

They gather corn and prepare the sacred tamales. There are wrapped in banana leaves and placed in front of the God Pots, also overnight, so the spirit of the Most High God can enter into the food.

They gather the sacred *copal* (incense) and place it in the God House so that it may be blessed by the gods.

And they gather the red achiote to be boiled into dye for the God Hats, and into thick paint for the final part of the four-day ceremony.

The sugar cane is taken from the God Hut and crushed in a wooden trough that looks much like a canoe. It is then leached with pure sugar water carried in a sacred jug by a priest who has washed his hands in the God Hut gourds three times. This leached "sweet water" is then transferred to the sacred *Chem*, a big canoe-like log that is never uncovered except to receive the sugar water from which the sacred drink is made. Strips of bark of the *balche* tree are put in the sugar water and it is allowed to ferment.

When the *balche*, as the sacred drink is called, the sacred tamales, the *copal* and the achiote dye are ready they are placed in the God Hut, the spirit of the Most High Supreme God is expected to come down through the God Pots and enter into the drink and into the food.

Before anything is eaten or drunk, it is once again offered ceremonially to the many gods. This is done by putting drops of the *balche* and particles of the tamales in the mouths of the God Pots, and also by sacrificing it up, down, and all around.

The purpose of the *Cuxuh* is to call down the spirit of the Most High God into man. The spirit enters the sacred drink and is consumed. The sacred spirit enters into the food and is eaten. When man drinks this drink and eats this food he is made into a god by capturing the god-spirit.

This spirit is then bound into man by putting on his head the red, achiote-dyed strips of special bark known as the "God Hat." Then finally all the participants are painted, together with the God Pots and the God Hut, with dots of the achiote dye which has been boiled down into a thick paste. These dots symbolize the jaguar—which is the representation of the earth form of the sun. This is another way of saying that the jaguar is the symbol of the eternal spirit pervading the universe.

The entire ceremony is performed by a high priest, an assistant priest, and, in this case, a four-year-old altar boy who kept the *copal* incense lighted atop the nine God Pots used in the ceremony.

All was in readiness. We had the camera equipment in perfect order and I was eagerly waiting to do the job I had come five thousand miles to do. Then the bottom fell out of my world!

I was told that the Lacandones absolutely refused to let a woman go into the God Hut. Not for any reason were women permitted in the God Hut during such a sacred ceremony. It was taboo!

I sat down and proved my femininity by bawling. Ruth comforted me and said very quietly, "Don't worry, Gene will fix everything."

On the morning the ceremony in the God Hut was to begin, the rain from a *norte* was falling in torrents. It was cold and dark. The wind and rain beat rhythmically on the grass roofs of the *champas*. The worst thing of all was the darkness.

The expedition had good cameras. But as a professional photographer I know what a camera can do. It was so dark inside the God Hut that it would be impossible to get color pictures with the film we had. Why, it was so dark that we couldn't see the men in the God Hut from our *champa*, which was only thirty paces away! Dr. Whitworth took the cameras and went into the God Hut. He lays no claim to being a professional photographer, and I had told him that it was useless to take pictures until the light got better. I suggested that he delay the ceremony.

But the ceremony started. And as the hours passed the rain grew more torrential. Then we started getting roll after roll of film, both 16-millimeter motion picture and 35-millimeter still film. I was heartsick.

During a pause in the ceremony Dr. Whitworth came down to our *champa* for a moment. We solemnly assured him that the film couldn't possibly be any good; the light was too poor. Besides in that 95% humidity the Urn would be covered with fungi that eat the emulsion and ruin the film. Such fungi developed very rapidly in such weather. So, even if it were properly exposed, the film would be no good. I assured him that he was wasting good film. He looked at me quite steadily in that strange way he has of seeing you and eternity all at the same time. Then he turned to Ruth.

"How about it, beautiful? Will the Boys let us down?"

"Never!"

"Don't worry, Mary. The film will be O.K.," he said. "It is God's business we do."

As a well-trained photographer, proud of my professional skill, I know that no film made for color could have taken those pictures in that darkness. I checked my own meter time and time again, and the readings called for a light-sensitivity far beyond that of any color film made. I could not have gotten those pictures. Yet I have been privileged to sit in front of a screen during lectures on the trip and see almost perfect pictures made under those impossible conditions. How was it done? I have no answer.

Yet another thing puzzles me. We walked amid all the dangers of that Green Hell with laughter on our lips because the Whitworths made it seem so easy and so simple. Terribly hard work became play. From somewhere we got boundless energy, which the work of the expedition required. Then another thing occurred. My worst hour arrived. My game left leg has a way of giving out. The nerves shut off and the muscles won't behave. Now this happened to me in the middle of a big push, when we were on a very tight schedule to get to a place of safety. I thought surely now they will send me back from the advance camp.

But I still didn't know the Whitworths. There was not one word of reproach for not confessing to them that I had a game leg before the expedition started, or for creating such a problem. As soon as they understood the situation Dr. Whitworth knelt beside me and touched me with the most soothing hands I've ever known. He massaged my leg from hip to heel with short, relaxing little strokes. In five minutes the pain was gone. After thirty minutes of rest I was up and moving, still carrying my own pack and equipment. By the next morning I felt better than I had for years. Even now I'm not having the trouble with that leg I formerly had.

For a while I thought might be fooling myself. But I saw Dr. Whitworth work another "miracle" cure. We met a woman who had not been able to turn her head to the right for thirty-five years. Imagine how she felt about the man who, in five minutes, took her pain away and made it possible for her to turn her head.

How was it that our expedition was able to go so far, do so much, and come through so many dangers with no more than a split fingernail? As I said, this puzzles me. Doria and Bruce were as amazed as I, for they were accustomed to jungle "happenstances." Three days after arriving, on April 11, 1959, to the safety of his home, one of our members broke his ribs in a fall from a tame horse. A letter from another member to Dr. Whitworth reads: "As long as we were with you I was perfectly well. But I was sick within three days after leaving you, and it was very bad for two weeks."

While we were with them the Whitworths seemed to radiate a perfect protection. During two-and-a-half months in the Green Hell, we were without so much as a sick day or a scratch. By then we all were ready to accept Ruth's explanation: "God walks with his arm around our shoulders."

Where Gene and Ruth go, there goes peace, happiness, laughter, well-being, and the presence of God. What makes it that way? I would like to find out. When I ask them, they only smile—and go on working miracles.

MYSTERY PAINTING IN ST· LOUIS JAIL

H· N· Ferguson

On a raw March morning in 1932 a cold, wind-driven rain whipped around the corners of the gray, forbidding building which is the Central Police Station in St. Louis, Mo. The Department janitor was making fast work of his task of cleaning the cells.

He entered the section of the jail officially known as the "Men's Holdover"—a segregated area where drunks picked up during the night found asylum until morning. The janitor entered Cell Number 8—and stopped dead in his tracks. With mouth agape, he stared fixedly at a beautiful life-size drawing of the Crucified Christ sketched on the bleak cell wall.

So began what has proved to be one of the great unsolved mysteries of the St. Louis Police Department.

For in the twenty-seven years that have passed since that morning the Department has been unable to determine the identity of the artist who drew this remarkable picture. Perhaps he is now long dead. At any rate he has made no effort to come forth and receive the plaudits that await him from the thousands of persons who have marveled at the genius displayed in his mysterious work of art.

Perhaps he has good reason for remaining anonymous. It may be that he has no desire to receive recognition for a painting conceived in such surroundings. Perhaps he is afflicted with the knowledge that never again could he hope to attain such heights. Or perhaps the elusive artist just doesn't care.

Thousands of eager sightseers have visited Cell Number 8 just to gaze upon the life-like picture inscribed upon its wall. The drab, iron-barred room has become a shrine. To prevent it from being damaged by enthusiastic visitors, and to preserve the work against possible fading, it has been covered by a plate.

Not only the curious find their way to the cell. Many art experts have studied the drawing. But not even the best of them has been able to determine the materials used by the artist in his work. They were not long in ruling out the most likely materials—such as oils, chalk, pencil, crayon, or water colors. They only shake their heads in bewilderment and admit their inability to name the material used.

Of course, the greatest mystery of all is the artist himself. What sort of genius could produce such a masterful piece of work under such hopeless conditions? The Police Department assigned some of its best men to the case. A search of the jail records has given no clue to the identification of the artist who occupied the cell.

The peculiar thing is that no single individual ever spent more than a few brief hours in the detention cell at one time. Obviously, if the work was completed in one visit, the artist had to work with unbelievable speed. But the intricate detail of the drawing seems to eliminate such a conclusion. A more reasonable assumption is that the artist was confined in the cell on several occasions before completing his work. But if this is true, how did the painting remain hidden from the eyes of the department janitor until its completion?

Today the identity of the artist is as much a mystery as it was in 1932. But a fantastic surmise has been advanced as to the materials used.

"The contention now is," says Colonel Jeremiah O'Connell, Chief of Police in St. Louis, "that the material composition of the Christ Crucified masterpiece is nothing more than a rubber heel and burnt matches. But," he adds cautiously, "this has not been definitely established."

TWO WATCHES STOPPED FOR DEATH

David Faubion

I often heard my older sisters speak of the way our mother could "see things before they happened," but not until after her untimely death did the real meaning of those remarks become clear to me.

My family was of rather modest means, and before my birth my father had taken up, in 1906, a homestead along the Barlow Trail in what was then a wilderness area of Oregon. Busy highway U.S. 26 now runs through the little settlement that bears our family name. There I was born and lived to late childhood. Mother often confided in me because, as she said, I was the only one she could talk to without being ridiculed. Ridicule does so much damage to the soul of the mocker, she said, she did not want to be the cause of harm to the soul of another. I have regretted all my life that I was too young to grasp all she told me about the "unseen," "the other side of life," and the many other "planes" of the "real."

When Grandmother died Mother received a small share of the estate. She used a part of the money to buy a good wristwatch. She wore this watch continually until the night of her death. The round, gold Waltham always had a special meaning to me, perhaps because of the way Mother had acquired it. The watch had become more a part of her than any of her other simple possessions. I was very happy when my father handed it to me to keep. Since it was not a small watch, by replacing the cloth band with one of leather its plain design became masculine enough in appearance so that I could wear it.

Several years after Mother's death in April, 1928, I married the daughter of a prominent Oregon political figure, Harry Lane. Years before, on the eve of his election to the United States Senate, he had traded an engraved gold watch, which he had carried since his graduation from medical school, to a dear and lifelong friend with this remark, "Mac, I've always wanted that plain, simple little watch because it's more in keeping with my way of life." The plain, simple life he led earned him the affection of his colleagues in the Senate who referred to him warmly as the Homespun Senator. His ability to foresee future events amazed those close to him. He became one of the "Willful Five", so-called by Woodrow Wilson because they voted against our participation in World War I. The hard-fought Senate battle in those hectic days in 1917 and the ensuing criticism of his heroic stand hastened his death, and his simple thin-cased Elgin watch eventually became mine also.

Early in 1945 my wife, Nina Lane Faubion, was stricken with cancer. She had traveled in the Andes Mountains from 1925 until 1929, collecting archeological relics and was warned at that time by the Indians of the Andes that if she entered the caves of the ancient peoples and disturbed their tombs she would die of cancer. This prophecy was now to be fulfilled.

We lived in Azalea, a small town in a rather isolated part of the state, and because of World War II it was impossible to get an ambulance and a hospital room at the same time for weeks on end. That was the most difficult time of my life. Not because of the twenty-four-hour watch I kept at my wife's bedside, but because of my helplessness to bring her some degree of comfort or a moment of relief from pain. There can be but one Source from which a cancer patient draws the strength to endure the suffering that is beyond the imagination of those who have not seen experienced it. The will to live in those last days would seem to stem from a knowledge that a miracle is at hand to drive the beast from the body, and that life must be clung to until the miracle is manifest. So it was with my wife, while I, though in perfect health, was rapidly weakening from mental anguish and lack of sleep.

One night, shortly after midnight, as I sat in my bedside chair, I was sure that the limits of my endurance had been reached. My wife's agonized cries pounded on every inch of my body, pleading for the help I could not give. I felt that the end was at hand for us both and was trying to fight back welcoming thoughts of it when my mother appeared before me. With a radiant smile, she held her arms outstretched as if to lay hands on the throbbing foreheads before her. Then she vanished. When I turned to look at my wife she was breathing evenly in sound sleep. I sank back into the chair and did not awaken until the telephone rang at 8:30 a.m. It was the ambulance company telling me that a hospital room was available and though it was Sunday they were ready to move my wife. We left for the Eugene hospital, 155 miles away at 11:30 a.m.

I rode at my wife's side in the back of the ambulance. She talked about some of the interesting places we had seen in our travels and mentioned the many times we had been over this road together. Then she slept. Just before reaching the hospital I looked at my mother's watch. It read 2:05 p.m. I knew it was later than that.

I drew my father-in-law's watch from my pocket and it too read 2:05.

We went on to the hospital and I saw to it that nothing was left undone for my wife's comfort.

The next morning, after checking with our doctors, I took the timepieces to a reputable watch maker. When he opened them he found that both balance shafts, the very hearts of the watches, were completely shattered. They were repaired at once and I hastened back to the hospital.

As I entered the room my wife greeted me with a smile and informed me that she had suffered no pain since we left home.

I made it a point to be close by from then on, especially in the afternoons. I read to her each day and she seemed to enjoy every hour that passed. Thursday afternoon she interrupted my reading. "I saw a very lovely woman the night before we left home," she said. "It would seem that it was your mother."

Those were her last words.

Both watches read 2:05 p.m.

THE POLTERGEIST THAT CAN WRITE

H. S. H. Chibbett

Thirty odd years ago, one of the most violent poltergeist hauntings in history took place in Eland Street, Battersea, South London. Today, another poltergeist is active just a few hundred yards away. It began in February, 1956, and its initial stages correspond closely with those of the earlier case. There were raps, fires, and objects moving through the air.

A psychic paper reported in May, 1956, that: "South London's poltergeist now has official recognition as 'baffling': A whole series of minor fires have occurred by the machinations of the poltergeist at Lavender Hill, at the home of an eighteen-year-old Shirley Irene Hitching. Firemen and detectives scoured the premises, people and possibilities. For yet another time their resultant communiqué was terse: 'baffled.'"

The disturbances—alarming as they sound—at first followed the normal trend of such affairs. Whenever such manifestations occur—and they are more common than you may suspect—the phenomena usually develop along recognized lines. There are loud raps or loud bangs, the smashing of crockery and the tilting or overthrow of heavy furniture. Sometimes stones are thrown; on other occasions objects are seen to move through the air by themselves, sometimes quite slowly and without damage to the articles or persons present.

Almost always an adolescent is nearby when the phenomena occur and there is a perhaps natural tendency to assume that the occurrences are in some way connected with the children. Furthermore, rarely is an object seen to start its trip through the air. Usually it is already in motion when first observed.

Poltergeist disturbances are international; they take place in all countries, but it is interesting that they occur most frequently in civilized communities such as England, the U.S.A., and Germany. The word *poltergeist* is a German word meaning "noisy ghost."

Today, three years after the start of these extraordinary phenomena in Battersea, there is still no sign that they are going to cease. This in itself is unusual, because normally the phenomena reach a peak within a few weeks and then die away as mysteriously as they began. But even as recently as

February of this year, wanton damage amounting to several hundred dollars was done to furniture and clothing.

Apart from the usual poltergeist activities, there have been phenomena which indicate intelligence behind the manifestations. Early in 1956 a simple alphabetical code was devised whereby the rapping sounds were used to convey messages from an "entity" who claimed to have lost his life by drowning in the English Channel. This communicator became known to the family as "Donald," because he said he resembled a near neighbor of the Hitchings' who had gone abroad.

In May, 1956, the entity objected to being called Donald, and said that he was really Louis XVII, younger son of Louis XVI and Marie Antoinette of France, both of whom were guillotined in 1793 during the French Revolution. This claim was received very skeptically by the Hitching family and all concerned. Nevertheless, from that time to the present, he has not deviated from his claim to be Louis XVII, who became Dauphin of France in 1789 on the death, at Meudon, of his elder brother, Louis-Joseph.

The poltergeist could not have chosen a more controversial figure than that of the ill-used young Dauphin. There is no lack of information regarding his life up to the year 1793, when he was imprisoned with his family in the Temple at Paris. It is generally assumed that he died in the arms of a gaoler named Etienne Lasne, in 1795, two years after the death of his parents at the guillotine.

After his alleged death rumors spread that the Dauphin had not really died in the Temple at all, but had escaped as far back as 1793 or even earlier. Numerous theories were voiced, among them one that a substitution had been effected and that another child resembling Louis XVII had taken his place and that it was this child who had died in the Temple. Therefore the real heir to the throne must still be alive and free.

The mystery deepened when public opinion belatedly demanded that the grave of the alleged prince be opened to establish the real facts. The first search—in 1817—yielded nothing. A coffin tallying with the official description was found but it was empty.

In the year 1846 fresh excavations were made in the churchyard of Sainte-Marguerite. Among the coffins disinterred was the one previously opened in 1817. When the coffin was reopened, it was found to contain a skeleton, the skull of which had actually been dissected. A doctor Recamier made a report on the remains in which he stated that the skeleton was that of a child about fifteen years old.

Later, in 1894, the remains were again exhumed and examined by a

Doctor Backer. He reported that the skeleton was that of a child at least fourteen years old.

According to Madal, one of the nearly two hundred writers on Louis XVII: "To this day it has been impossible to find the skeleton of a ten-year-old Dauphin on the spot where he was supposed to have been buried." This is, of course, historically accurate. The Dauphin was born on March 27, 1785, and is supposed to have died in the Temple on June 8, 1795, when he would have been ten years, three months old.

It would appear, therefore, that whoever was buried as Louis XVII, Duc de Normandie, was not the boy-king himself. Because of the uncertainty, no fewer than thirty pretenders claimed to be the Dauphin at the restoration of the French Monarchy. Chief among these was Karl Wilhelm Naundorff. He produced evidence of his identity as the younger son of Louis XVI which convinced even his governess, Mme. de Rambaud, Louis XVI's last Minister of Justice, M. July, and many others who had known the young prince intimately.

Whatever the facts may have been, there is little doubt that the real Dauphin did not die in the Temple prison in Paris in 1795.

Let us now revert to the entity at Battersea which manifested first as a typical poltergeist and then announced itself as Louis XVII. Do we get a clear enough picture of a royal personage returned from the grave to prove that he was the lineal descendant of the House of Bourbon?

The answer at present must be "No." For, although his messages contain masses of data about the period of the French Revolution, they are interspersed with much irrelevant material and a predilection for modern affairs that accords with Shirley Hitching's own character. Yet it cannot be denied that this entity exhibits personal qualities which are more appropriate to Louis XVII than to Shirley. Its reaction to frustration, its imperious self-esteem, its decided indiscretion, are all more typical of the Dauphin than of the Battersea teenager.

On April 15, 1956, a message said, "I come to tell what I look like— five foot high, fair head, blue eyes, thirty-five wide" (presumably around the chest).

At about this time an increase in the physical phenomena. The house was full of reporters and investigators of all kinds, and abnormal things were happening every day. The Hitching family was in a state of turmoil and fear. At night they used to huddle together on the kitchen floor, keeping a weather eye open for mysterious fires and gas taps which somehow were turned on full. Many of the messages were threats to set fire to the house, and peremptory orders to get this or that. Any refusal to obey instructions was met by further threats, or retaliatory action.

Nearly three weeks later came the first definite claim that the "personification" was Louis XVII, son of Louis XVI and Marie Antoinette. He said that his father and mother had died on the guillotine, and that he had been drowned in the English Channel. He added that his dress was "satin, a tail coat, knee breeches, hose, lace waistcoat, black buckle shoes." He continued, "Some wore wigs."

On May 19, 1956, the entity stated, "I am Donald in this age..." (remember the poltergeist was christened "Donald" by the family because of his resemblance to a neighbor) "...I am originally Louis XVII, son of Louis XVI, of the House of Bourbon." A similar message was repeated on the following day, with the addition, "I know French."

There is a first reference to a request for "ten silver pieces" on May 26, and the next day an admonitory message to Shirley: "If you had to iron the shirts I wore, with lace frills, you would moan!"

On May 28 he said, "Clothes have changed, but the way of life has not. I know more about life than you know. I was born before you. I can tell you all about Jacko the monkey, and how Connie would run and hide when in trouble. She had long flowing hair."

One sees an intriguing picture of the life of a young French prince. Was Jacko the monkey a pet at the French Court at Versailles Palace? Who was Connie, with the long flowing hair? Could the subconscious or conscious mind of a young girl be responsible for all this?

About this time other phenomena began. The sitting room already had been commandeered by "Donald" for his own use, and was littered with dolls dressed as Marie Antoinette and other royal personages, attired by Shirley under "Donald's" express directions. Now drawings began to appear on the walls, some of shields with crossed swords superimposed. There were fleurs-de-lis on the shields and underneath the words: *Roi Louis*. Shirley denied having made these drawings. As time went on, more fleurs-de-lis appeared on the bedroom walls, ceilings and elsewhere.

During this same period many messages arrived giving historical names and dates. Exhaustive research has shown that the majority of these are correct but of little evidential value since the information could have been gleaned from any history of the period. However, Shirley does not belong to a library and there are no books in the house on the period. She did not take French history at school, according to her school certificates.

On May 31 "Donald" asked, "Do you know what the guillotine was?

You have one ... the block. They both do the same thing."

Referring to one of the dolls in "his" room, "Donald" gave these instructions on June 2, 1956: "Let us give that doll a French Royal formal name ... *Oui* ... let us think ... let it be Marie Antoinette, the name of *ma mere*. It must be her for she has a French face. Let me put the flurdeley (*fleur-de-lis*) on her, because my mother had it branded. Will you dress Marie as I describe: she must have six petticoats, two skirts, a top—you know, her hair all curls, a fan, shoes, the top square neck, long sleeves with lace edges—lots of lace—silk too. If you dress her for me, I get the pleasure. I will help in describing. You can look in pictures. Please do this for me..."

A note of mine made at the time says: "Recent messages convey an impression of a young boy, imperious in his demands on Shirley's time and attention, eager to show off, and rather shaky in his spelling. Interesting, too, is the increasing use of French words, and also the reference on May 31 to the block, when he says: 'you have one.' Evidently 'Donald' is not yet aware that the method of execution in England nowadays has changed."

Concurrently, typical poltergeist activity continued. On the evening of June 10, 1956, the following phenomena occurred: Shirley's clothes disappeared and were eventually found stowed away in the piano, thrust down among the wires. Then, while Shirley and her parents were all together in the dining room, a knife was thrown from the kitchenette and stuck in the window frame of the dining room. At 10:30 p.m. the family went to bed. At this period they all shared the same bedroom. Disturbances occurred almost at once. The bedclothes were disarranged, there were violent scratching sounds, and raps as though on metal.

Suddenly Shirley called out that there was something "furry" at the foot of the bed. Investigation disclosed that there was a whole mass of red flock in her bed; and when the quilt was examined, several slits were found in it, as though caused by a penknife or scissors. On the face of it, the red flock had been extracted from the interior, though how this could have been done in such a short period of time is a mystery. There were several slits but none large enough for the flock to be extracted quickly, in quantity. Normally it would have had to be "teased" out bit by bit as the bundle of flock was half a foot in diameter. Following this, Shirley refused to remain in the bed and spent the night in a wicker chair.

During the night, a pair of scissors was thrown at Mr. Walter Hitching. While Shirley was dressing in the morning a screwdriver was thrown at Mrs. Catherine Hitching who was still in bed. It hit her a glancing blow on the back. In the kitchen, a boiling kettle was overturned, and then another narrowly missed scalding Shirley's feet.

The flood of messages ran into many hundreds. They covered all sorts of subjects from Latin tags to horse-race winners, and indifferent French was on the increase. Sometimes English, French and Latin appeared in the same sentences. Fleur-de-lis occurred mysteriously in all sorts of places. On one occasion, the writer was looking at a fleur-de-lis impression on the shoulder of the doll dressed as Marie Antoinette. I expressed a wish aloud that "Donald" would show me how these were made. A few minutes later I was with the family in the dining room. Shirley was standing by the fireplace and her parents were seated. All three were in full view. Suddenly Shirley's mother exclaimed: "What is that on your arm, Shirley?"

On the upper part of her bare left arm was the imprint of a small, dark-blue fleur-de-lis. It looked as though it had been drawn or stamped there with indelible ink. As far as I had noticed, Shirley had made no untoward movement. I examined her closely to see whether there were any more impressions visible on her. There were none. I watched her movements closely thereafter. However, a few minutes later there was another similar mark—this time on the right side of her neck. I am reasonably certain that neither she nor her parents could have made this without my knowledge. I searched the room but could find no trace of any instrument which could have made the impressions.

At this early stage of the investigation, Shirley and her parents had no previous knowledge of parapsychological phenomena. Yet on Wednesday, June 27, when I visited the house I was informed that "Donald" had left a sealed envelope for me on a coffee table in "his" room. On a settee were the dolls which Shirley had dressed in accordance with "Donald's" instructions, Marie Antoinette was posed as though sitting on a throne, and the other dolls, purporting to be Lady Jane Grey, Anne Boleyn, etc., were placed round her in curtseying positions. Shirley assured me that "Donald" had placed them so.

The envelope contained a local paper. On page nine there was some writing in ink. This seemed indecipherable at first, but when held to a mirror it read: "Out in one month. Don't worry, Shirley." This promise to go was not kept, but the interesting point is that the message was in "mirror" writing. The Hitching family was unaware that "mirror-writing" is relatively common in written psychic communications. There was an error in the spelling of the word "month" which showed that the sender was "Donald", whose rapped messages contained the same error.

On June 24, 1956, "Donald" rapped out to Shirley:

"Can you fence? It is rare in girls, but I could teach you. I knew how to handle a sword when I was only ten. You had to defend yourself in my day. It was peaceful until the Revolution came." "Donald" continued to give detailed fencing instructions. According to a note made by Shirley, "Donald" said that he—as Louis XVII—was left-handed.

"Donald's" instructions seem remarkably accurate, and unlikely to be part of the general knowledge of a working-class adolescent like Shirley. In fact, one gets an oddly disturbing picture of a youth who might actually have experienced these things.

From time to time, "Donald" appeared to feel frustrated and one of his communications to Shirley said, "I am sad ... disappointed. I want it to be as it was in my palace—this room; I have got my dolls but I am lonely. I have no swords hanging on the walls. The furniture is not right. I have never seen any like it. My work is taking too long. It should have been done by now."

Again on June 28, 1956, he said, "Shirley, when I was young I played with toys. Everyone said I was mad; but I loved my little soldiers, dolls all dressed in scarlet, blue, yellow, gold, silver, black and white. It is not wrong to have a secret—I loved to play with dolls like you. I was sick of being pushed about, of talks with governesses, fencing lessons, dancing. All I wanted was to be free—no state laws. I loved France though, but I was not happy in Court. Boys would take my punishment if I was bad—why couldn't they let me take my own punishment like a man? To hell with the Court of France. That is why I must tell people how lucky they are now."

One of the most interesting accounts given by the alleged Louis XVII was a description of his life at Court.

"I would like to tell you of Versailles—my life there. It was grand. Do you know, my Nanette would take me round the garden every morning, and we always stopped to see the birds. My father and grandfather had peacocks and turkeys—not like English ones. They had blue heads with red spots on them, and green feathers with yellow and blue on their wings—beautiful. There were some doves, pigeons, lyre birds with big fan tails. We had seventy-nine peacocks, but they were killed in the Revolution to feed old Robespierre and his rats. But in the days of goodness, my father let me in Court after my brother died. I was the center of attraction. I was allowed at Court with the nobility and gentry—the French and Austrian friends of my father and mother were all so charming at Versailles.

"I had my own room. I had a map all over the floor like a carpet, of France of course; and I had little houses—chateaux—also I had a toy gun which fired spears, and loads and loads of toy soldiers in their shiny paint. They were wonderful. I also had my own desks to do my lessons on. Do you know, I got up at nine o'clock and had a man servant to dress me. Then Nickolos sometimes crept up to see me in my suite of rooms. We would talk till he had to go."

So the torrent of rapped messages continued week in and month out, a mass of communications which, for this period alone, must run into many thousands of words. They were received in a mixture of French and English.

During this whole period manifestations of various kinds occurred, until on August 13, 1956, "Donald" sent the following message to Mr. Hitching: "I want a pen that you put black water (ink) in and it writes. Not a quill pen. I want one like Shirley has got. I can keep my own diary like I used to."

A notebook and fountain pen were duly provided, and new phenomena began to appear. Long straggling characters sprawled across pages were barely decipherable as words.

At 2:00 p.m. on October 17, 1956, the following rapped message was received by Shirley: "I want a sweet—do you? If I was in France I would have a *dragee*. It is almond in sugar. They cost about two sous. If I go to France again I will go to 28, Rue du Baal, Paris, and get you one. I was given a box of *dragees* when I was baptized ... do you want some if I get one? The Seugnot family were the makers of those lovely *dragees*. I do not know of Mme. Seugnot now. She had a daughter and two sons. The daughter was called Marie, and the sons, Perrie and Paul. But the shop is still there. I think M. and Mme. Seugnot were guillotined for being Royalist, but their children lived."

A colleague of mine went to Paris in due course but was unable to find any such road.

I then wrote to the English representatives of the French Chamber of Commerce, giving what details I had and enquiring whether from their records of French sweetmeat makers they could confirm the contemporary existence of a firm under the name of Seugnot, or whether there ever was such an address as Rue du Baal in the years 1785 to 1793.

Much to my astonishment, the reply I received June 11, 1958 read: "Thank you for your letter ... concerning a shop at 28, Rue du Bac, Paris 17e. Upon enquiry, I have pleasure in advising you that there still exists at the above address a sweetshop with the heading of Seugnot."

Even if the entity had not got the spelling right, this was still quite remarkable.

Next I wrote to Mons. Seugnot, Confiseur-Chocolatier, 28, Rue du Bac. I mentioned that the royal family of Louis XVI, before they were imprisoned in the Tower, were accustomed to purchase their *dragees* from the Seugnot family of that era; and that M. and Mme. Seugnot were said to have perished on the guillotine as Royalists. Could he confirm this, together with the statement that two sons and one daughter survived?

A free translation of M. Seugnot's reply dated June 21 says: "The information which you have given me is correct. I am going to make some enquiries into historical records for further details, and you may have to wait some weeks; but I thought I would let you know now, so that you will not be surprised at any delay."

No further letter has been received from M. Seugnot as yet. And knowing the circumstances of Shirley's home life I find it very difficult to believe that she could have obtained the detailed information supplied by the poltergeist.

It was in the fall of 1956 that a sealed and addressed envelope was found on the coffee table in "Donald's" room. At "Donald's" request it was posted to me. And on the morning of November 1, 1956, I received what is possibly the first letter ever posted from a poltergeist. It was the forerunner of an ocean of correspondence mailed to myself and to many other persons. It still continues at the present time.

And I am puzzled, now as then. Am I the recipient, through Her Majesty's Mail, of letters from a poltergeist, from a clever Shirley Hitching, or from His Royal Highness, Prince Louis Charles Philippe, Duc de Bourbon?

MY VOYAGE TO ETERNITY

Etna Elliot

"**H**old to the lion's ruff," said Jesus, "and follow me." That is what he told me.

I was just out of the hospital after undergoing a major operation, and the doctors had told my family that it would be necessary for me to undergo a second operation before I could be well again.

When I blew out the light in the little kerosene lamp on that blistering hot California night in 1929, my heart was breaking; my body seemed made of lead and I did not think I could possibly face another day.

As I got quietly into bed beside my restless husband my heart went out to him, for I knew the burden he was carrying. We had three children and very little food in the house and did not know where the next week's supply would come from. We were living in a little shack on a mining claim in El Dorado County near Auburn, where my husband was prospecting, trying to find a little gold or take out a pocket, as he called it.

"Oh, God!" I prayed, "What can we do? Oh! What can we do? Show me the way. There must be a way."

I lay there in the hot, sticky darkness with my eyes wide open. My husband and children all were sleeping; I could hear their even breathing and I thought, "Oh, God! Give them a break; they are deserving."

Finally I became quiet and rested. I felt cool and comfortable for the first time in weeks. In a sort of semiconscious sleep I was fully aware of my home surroundings and all the little noises of the night. I could hear the dog moving around outside and, at the same time, I suddenly felt myself standing where it was very cold and dark.

Before me was a great iron fence at least eight feet high; each iron rod in it was about four inches apart. There was a great gate there, tightly closed, and on the other side of the fence from me were scores of people. They were the most terrible people; wild, gaunt, ragged people, some without eyes, some without teeth and hair, crippled, deformed, mean, savage people, all very tall, towering above me and all reaching through that iron fence trying to get at me. It seemed as if they all hated me and wanted to tear me apart. The whole dark, terrible scene closed around me with an unknown terror.

I remember it very clearly!

For some reason not known to me I had to go through that gate. I *had* to get on the other side of that fence. As I would step toward the gate, the terrible people would all make a wild, screaming lunge for me, stretching their arms through the bars, trying to reach me.

I was numb with fear but I had to get through. I thought, "Oh! If I could only wake my husband." For I still was conscious of his presence in bed beside me at the same time that I was standing alone in that cold, windy darkness, facing that insane mob of inhuman people.

"Oh, God," I cried, "what will I do?"

Then I heard a voice, a very familiar voice it seemed, a kind, loving, sweet voice say, "Fear not."

And then I saw him. Oh! The wondrous beauty of that scene and what followed. If I could only tell you what I saw and felt, if I could just give you one glimpse of the dear face of Jesus! But I can only try to tell you as nearly as possible since there are no words to express what I saw and heard and did.

I could now see Him plainly in his bright-colored robe, standing on the other side of the fence from me, behind and above this crowd of people. There was a shining radiance all about him and a beautiful smile on his face—the sweetest, loving smile I ever have seen on a face! The other people did not seem to hear or see him; they still reached for me. I looked over their heads and up at Jesus and he reached His hand out to me and said, "Hold to the lion's ruff." Instantly beside me was a monstrous lion. He rubbed against my body like a huge kitten.

All my fear vanished. The cold wind stopped blowing and I was warm and comfortable. Jesus, reached His hand out to me and said again, "Just hold to the lion's ruff."

I placed my right hand on the giant lion's neck and into his big, fluffy mane, as I had always called it. When Jesus called it the lion's ruff, that was the first time I had ever heard it called so.

I got a good handhold and hung onto that blessed lion, then I looked up at Jesus and He was smiling. His smile gathered me in and made me one with him. He beckoned for me to come to Him and said in that very gentle voice, "Now, just hold to the lion's ruff and follow me." Then the gigantic lion and I started walking toward that gate and all that mob of terrible people. They all were lunging and reaching out with clawing hands, trying to get hold of me, when the lion gave a terrible roar. He first turned his head to one side, then to the other, roaring each time. The gate began to swing open and back, pushing the mob of screaming people back and behind it. They still did not see nor hear Jesus, but they did see the lion and were afraid. They drew back, cringing behind those bars, stumbling back into the darkness.

We walked through that gate to Jesus waiting on the other side with that same sweet smile. He beckoned me to follow Him and as He turned I noticed for the first time that He carried a cane or rod as high as His head. It had a crook or elbow at the top and was so shiny that it blended in with the radiance all about Him.

He started walking up a steep narrow trail that shone so brightly it looked like a trail of bright, shiny mirrors.

The lion and I were right behind Him, I still clutching the lion's ruff. At first it seemed I could not lift my feet, they were so heavy and I was so tired and the trail was so steep, but as we advanced up that trail I became light as a feather and moved with little or no effort. The lion seemed so happy at this improvement that he frolicked like a pup.

Now Jesus was drawing a little farther ahead of me but at every little bend in the trail He would stop and turn to beckon me on and up that bright, narrow trail with Him. This trail wound up through the sky just like a trail winds up a mountain. On each side of the trail was a beautiful blue mist or vapor.

At last Jesus entered into such a bright radiance that He was fading from my sight. Just before He vanished He turned again and beckoned me to follow. He stood holding His staff and watched me for a minute or so with that clear look on His face that I have seen on the face of young mothers as they watch their babies wobbling on their tiny legs for the first time.

I was still conscious of my earthly surroundings. Yet, I was on that trail with the lion, in the bright light of Jesus. Then I felt my fingers release the lion's ruff and his great body moved reluctantly away from mine.

I found myself sitting upright in bed watching the trail and that bright light and the shadowy lion all disappear into a fading mist. I sat there motionless for I don't know how long, Watching the wall as if it were a blank movie screen.

I cannot remember any sensation or feeling. I seemed to be in a daze, not even conscious of having a body. I got quietly out of bed, put on robe and slippers and went out into the night under the bright moon and stars. I looked up at the sky and tears began to fall. I could not stop them. I felt lonely and sad and I also felt a deep quiet joy, a special kind of joy I never had felt before. I felt free and safe and for the first time in years I felt the blessedness of security!

I had acted upon the word of Jesus and held to the ruff of that heavenly lion and strength and courage had poured through me. I had walked unafraid to Jesus' side and followed Him to safety and freedom.

Now, where was my fear, my sick, weak body, my dark, dreary thoughts, my sad, heavy heart? Somewhere on that trail with Jesus they all had vanished, leaving me free, clean, and whole. I now knew that I would follow Jesus on into eternity. I would never again be afraid.

Day was now breaking. The birds began to twitter and move about in the trees. I have often wondered if my feet were touching the ground as I faced that beautiful morning sunrise. I was so happy I could have shouted, although I found myself very quiet, as if the whole world must be hushed before the majesty of what I had seen.

I returned to the cabin, dressed quietly and started breakfast. The family awakened and all flocked to the kitchen, as usual. As their eyes fell upon me they stopped, they looked and they saw the miracle that had taken place. It shone in my face, the tilt of my head, the lift of my shoulders. I hadn't noticed before, but I was standing up straight for the first time in months.

I tried to tell them where I had been, what I had seen and done, but to this day I don't think they heard a word I was saying. They just stared at me.

My mother arrived at the cabin about noon, as was her daily habit, expecting to find me worse, as she had each day before. To her great astonishment, I had a large wash drying on the line and was preparing lunch for the family.

As she stepped out of the car I came to the cabin door and said "I am healed." And I threw my arms around her and lifted her right off the ground.

I can tell you now that I never had that second operation. And not only was I healed but I felt ten years younger, and for days I had the sensation of walking on air.

My husband found his pocket just a few days after my walk up that trail with Jesus. Some of the quartz in the rich vein was half gold and it assayed $1,586 per ton and there were many tons of it. No doubt many of you have seen specimens of our gold quartz for it was on exhibit at the California State Fair for several years and in many of our larger banks.

I followed Jesus from sickness and poverty into health and plenty, into peace and happiness. I was completely healed, for my doctor said, "I have seen several miraculous healings and this is one also."

Made in the USA
Las Vegas, NV
08 February 2022